Canada:
Profile of a Nation

John Molyneux
Head of Geography
Harbord Collegiate
Toronto, Ontario

Eric Jones
Geography Department
Central Technical School
Toronto, Ontario

McGRAW-HILL RYERSON LIMITED

Toronto   Montreal   New York   London   Sydney   Johannesburg
Mexico   Panama   Düsseldorf   Singapore   Sao Paulo
Kuala Lumpur   New Delhi

CANADA: PROFILE OF A NATION

ISBN 0-07-077463-3

2 3 4 5 6 7 8 9 10 AP 3 2 1 0 9 8 7 6 5 4

Printed and bound in Canada

Cover photographs, clockwise from upper left.

Fishing, Little Harbour, Nova Scotia: *Susan Kill*/British Columbia
Rockies: *Susan Kill*/Carnival, Quebec City: *Douglas Ashton*/
Toronto waterfront: *McCullagh Studio*/Farm machinery, Portage
la Prairie, Manitoba: *Susan Kill*/Eskimo family and dog team,
Contwoyto Lake, N.W.T.: *Don Crawley.*

Table of Contents

Note: A footnote number in an assignment refers to the corresponding appendix number.

Preface

To complete a study successfully takes an average class about two weeks. This time period allows for the illustration of the study by motion picture or film strip. A first-rate student might progress faster than the average but will find that the book represents a demanding and interesting year's work.

This book differs from other, conventional texts in several important respects. There is the much improved method of organizing geographical data as used by students at the high school level. The teacher is largely relieved of the time-consuming task of gathering material for lesson preparation. Instead, class time is used much more in resolving problems on a personal or individual basis. This results in weaker students being given more of the attention which they need. It is, in fact, possible to organize a course with this book so that students are able to learn at their own speed. Whether used in a rigidly formal program or in an open-plan classroom situation, the book has equal value, for the students have to do most of the work. They must draw all the maps, charts, and graphs. It is they who must present interpretations and reasoned conclusions. Testing and grading is thus greatly simplified.

We have found through experience that it is necessary to provide all the information that a student needs to complete an assignment. There is little or no value from the practical classroom point of view in setting a loosely structured library research assignment. Accordingly, the assignments in this book are based only on information available in the text, of which there is naturally a great deal.

Our statistics are metric of, course. They come from a wide variety of Canadian Government publications including the Canada Year Book, and the output of Statistics Canada. Data sources are as recent as possible.

The authors are currently teaching for the Toronto Board of Education, so that it is from the crucible of the classroom that our ideas and methods have come. Our approach has been refined over a period of several years and has met with enthusiastic responses from teachers and students alike.

We should like to thank our wives for their patience and forbearance while this manuscript was being prepared. Their interest and encouragement helped enormously.

EWJ
JEM
Toronto 1973

1 The Arctic

REGIONALISM

A dictionary definition of a region could well read something like: *region*, n, part of a country with more or less definitely marked characteristics; separate part of world.

Don't go any further into this study until you've done the first assignment! Don't go any further; didn't you read the notice? Don't . . .

1-1. It's a simple assignment, just to ease you into the idea gently. Write down the first ten things you think of when you hear the words *Arctic Canada*. That's right, ten.

Stop. Have you done the first assignment yet? If not, then go back and do it immediately.

You probably found that you had a bit of trouble thinking of *ten* things, didn't you? The first few were easy, then you had to think for the next few; but the last few . . .

That's one of the most important lessons about the Arctic that you've just learned. There isn't much there that you can instantly remember. There isn't much there. Not much that's positive, that is. There's plenty of negative data, though.

For example, one of the top items on your list was undoubtedly *coldness*, or some such negative word. There is a lot of coldness, but not much heat, and that's a pretty important characteristic of the Arctic. In fact, it's what really distinguishes the Arctic in particular from the Northland in general. The Arctic is that part of the Northland where it is too cold for trees to grow. This means that the Arctic is only the northernmost part of the Northland. The first things we have to do, then, in describing the character of the Arctic are (a) find out how cold it has to be before trees fail to grow, and (b) find out where this situation exists in northern Canada.

That's not quite so easy as it sounds. For example, trees don't fail to grow at any particular temperature; they do it bit by bit. So that at, say, a July monthly mean of about 15°C trees grow well, but at a July monthly mean of about 7.5°C trees don't grow at all. Somewhere between 15°C and 7.5°C trees fail to grow. But, as we said, they do it gradually: by the time temperatures (July monthly means all the time, of course) are down to about 11-12°C, trees are much smaller and much more widely spaced. The forest is no longer forest; it is more likely widely scattered stunted trees amidst a lot of bush. By the time temperatures are down to 10°C, trees have almost given up. Not quite, however, because we still find some of the hardier types (alder and willow, for example) growing in favoured localities, such as along well-drained river banks. These hardier types gradually disappear as you move northwards, so that by the time temperatures are down to 7-8°C there are no trees left. At these July temperatures you're well and truly in the Arctic, but just where exactly did you come in? Most people generally use the 10°C isotherm (July mean, of course) as the line of entry, partly because most trees have given up by then and partly because it's an easy figure to remember (so remember it!).

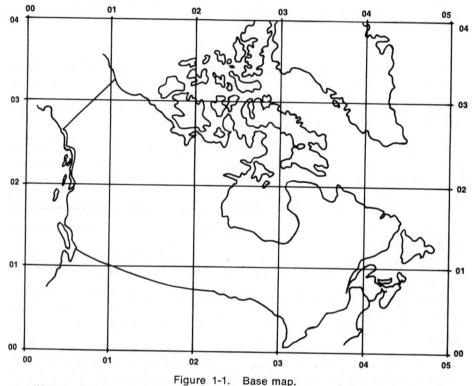

Figure 1-1. Base map.

1-2. Enlarge the map in Figure 1-1 to at least four times its size, together with all the grid markings and the figures. Then interpolate the 10°C mean July isotherm (on your copy, not in this book!). Shade all the land and sea which lies to the *south* of this line in either grey or black; it's an area we are not concerned with in this study, so we might just as well shade it out. In order to find out the run of the 10°C isotherm, plot the following references on to *your* map and join them up with a smooth curved line: from west to east — 009034 — 011031 — 013029 — 015028 — 017025 — 019024 — 021023 — 022022 — 023021 — 023020 — 024017 — 025015 — 028013 — 031013 — 032014 — 032017 — 034018 — 036018 — 039017 — 044016 — 046015. Use a bright colour.

The 10°C line merely marks in a generalized way the northernmost limits of tree growth (the so-called *tree line*), but it tells us nothing about what it's like north of the line (except that there aren't many trees there because it's too cold). If you want to get a clearer idea of temperatures in the Arctic, consider the following. Cambridge Bay (021027) has a maximum in July of 8°C and a minimum in February of −32°C, and it's fairly typical. Frobisher Bay (034023) has a maximum of 7.5°C and a minimum of −26°C, and Alert (Canada's most northerly settlement — a weather station — at 028040) has a maximum of 4°C and a minimum of −33°C. Throughout the Arctic, temperatures are never over 10°C on a mean monthly basis (though you may get the odd few days over 10°C), and they are usually below freezing for between eight to ten months each year. So now we know what cold means.

Another thing you probably had on your list as well as coldness was snow and ice. Wrong. There may be a bit of snow lying around in winter, and you may get the occasional blizzard, but there's not very much snow really. It just looks as though there's a lot because it doesn't melt away very much (remember: temperatures are usually below freezing for eight to ten months each year). In fact, most parts of the Arctic get less snow each year than most places farther south.

Canadian Arctic			Southern Canada		
	number of days	mean amount*		number of days	mean amount*
Alert	104	124 cm	Charlottetown	48	286 cm
Cambridge Bay	45	77 cm	Sydney	52	245 cm
Frobisher Bay	72	185 cm	Quebec	73	314 cm
Resolute	74	71 cm	Montreal	62	256 cm
Coral Harbour	71	105 cm	London	58	196 cm
			Ottawa	51	204 cm
			Thunder Bay	59	237 cm
			Toronto	45	139 cm
			Winnipeg	57	126 cm
			Calgary	54	145 cm
			Vancouver	12	62 cm

*denotes amount of snowfall, which may be divided by 10 to produce rainfall equivalent (i.e., recorded precipitation).

Figure 1-2.   Snowfall data for selected places in Canada.

1-3.   Plot average daily snowfall from Figure 1-2 as a vertical bar graph,' colouring the southern bars to contrast with the northern bars.

Why do you think precipitation is so low? It's low enough, indeed, for the Arctic to be considered a desert. Most places receive less than 25 cm a year, and that's a recognized limit for deserts. Again, consider these figures. Alert receives a total precipitation (winter snow plus summer rain) of 15 cm; Cambridge Bay gets 14 cm; Resolute (024032) has 13 cm; and Coral Harbour (028022) receives 22 cm. These are all quantities which would not be out of place in the Sahara desert (compare: Biskra 16 cm; Agades 17 cm; Touggourt 7 cm; Tamanrasset 4 cm). Why is precipitation so low? Well, the basic reason is the cold again. The air is so cold that it is incapable of holding moisture vapour, and so it cannot produce much precipitation under any conditions.

That makes it almost impossible to grow any crops in the Arctic, even assuming it was warm enough to do so. Indeed it's warm enough to grow, say, cabbages and potatoes. But you need to have irrigation water.

However, since irrigation water is scarce, farming is doubly discouraged. Indeed, there is not much that grows naturally, let alone for farmers. You get some stunted bushes, quite a bit of moss, lots of lichens (pronounced likens), and masses of summer flowers, but that's about all. The whole assembly is called *tundra* by specialists and the *barren lands* by almost everyone else.

Perhaps you even put tundra or barren lands down in your list. Good, if you did.

Did you put down *darkness*, too? It's one of the characteristics of lands within the Arctic Circle that they get lots of sunshine in summer (on some days — or even weeks, depending how far north you are — in summer, the sun doesn't set) and lots of darkness in winter (the sun not rising at all on some days — or weeks, depending how far north you are). The plentiful sunshine of summer permits cabbages and potatoes to grow (if you can get enough water for them), but the long winter darkness doesn't allow anything to grow. Even the people tend to go slightly crazy in the long darkness; they sit around indoors and try to think of things to do. They get what is called *cabin fever.*

Along with the cold and the darkness and the drought you might as well add in *permafrost*, if you haven't already got it on your list. The cold is so intense and so long-lasting that the ground below the surface never thaws at all. It is permanently frozen. The surface is different; it is frozen only in winter (eight to ten months, don't forget), but it thaws out in summer. When it thaws out, the water in the soil (if there is any soil) can't usually drain away very easily. Normally it would trickle down into the subsoil, but it can't in the Arctic because the subsoil is frozen, so it stays on the surface and forms swamps (called *muskeg*).

And that's only if there's any soil. Mostly there's just bare rock and sheets of stones (caused by frost breaking up the bare rock). It's not a land that encourages an easy life. Clearly, the people who live here cannot get together in large groups, because the land could not support them. Traditionally the family was the unit of survival, and life was earned (and earned is the right word!) by hunting and fishing. Herds of caribou wandering over the barren lands and living off the tundra could be hunted; fish in the rivers of summer and the sea-water of the year-round could be hunted; seals could be hunted; birds could be hunted; and Arctic mice, hares, and foxes could also be hunted. Life was very hard, although at times exciting.

Because the life was hard and the land was hard and the climate was hard,

Gulf Oil Canada

Scene in Arctic, near Inuvik.

the people were sparse. Population densities in the Arctic are amongst the lowest in the world, even though today the birth rate of the Eskimo is the highest in the world. In an area of about 2 500 000 square kilometres in the Arctic there are only about 20 000 people. The land is really empty!

	Area (square kilometres)	Population (numbers)
Canadian Arctic	2 500 000	20 000
Canada as a whole	9 961 140	22 000 000
Ontario	1 068 587	7 700 000
Prince Edward Island	5 656	112 000
U.S.A.	9 204 860	205 000 000
China	9 735 810	750 000 000
India	3 271 170	550 000 000
Italy	300 440	53 000 000

Figure 1-3.   Area and population data for selected regions.

1-4.   Plot the population densities which you calculate from the data in Figure 1-3 as an ordered horizontal bar graph.[1] *Emptiness* is not just a word; it's a way of life.

Yet another aspect of life in the Arctic is its *remoteness*. It's easy to think of the Arctic as "up in the north somewhere," but do you realise just how far north it really is?

	approximate air distance in kilometres
Edmonton (013014) to Inuvik (012031)	2 000
Winnipeg (022008) to Coppermine (017026)	2 200
Montreal (037005) to Alert (028040)	4 100
Montreal (037005) to Resolute (024032)	3 400
Calgary (012011) to Tuktoyaktuk (013031)	2 200
Edmonton (013014) to Cambridge Bay (021027)	1 800
Montreal (037005) to Frobisher Bay (034023)	2 100
Winnipeg (022008) to Resolute (024032)	2 700
Winnipeg (022008) to Edmonton (013014)	1 200
Winnipeg (022008) to Montreal (037005)	1 800
Calgary (012011) to Montreal (037005)	3 000
Inuvik (012031) to Frobisher Bay (034023)	2 900
Frobisher Bay (034023) to Alert (028040)	2 100

Figure 1-4.   Distances between selected settlements.

1-5. Very easy. But let's hope it puts the concept of distances across to you. Draw lines to scale (as on a horizontal bar graph) to show the distances quoted in Figure 1-4.

Even when you get to the Arctic there are still vast distances to cross. After all, the Arctic runs from the extreme west of Canada to the extreme east, and that's a long way even in the south. But within the Arctic you face the additional problems of lack of roads (there aren't any), lack of railways (there aren't any), lack of waterways (they are usually frozen), lack of coastal shipping (the waters are usually frozen), and even nowadays a lack of dog-teams, because the Eskimos don't go in for hunting much now. The main way to get around is by air, and all the tiny scattered settlements have at least a single airstrip. However, fog, low cloud, blizzards, blowing snow, and drifting snow often close down the tiny airstrips, even during the daylight months. So people don't get many outside visitors.

And not everyone has a plane either. The ones who don't usually have to rely on snowmobiles, and these have now mostly displaced the old huskies. The best time for getting around is naturally winter — not only because of the snowmobiles but also (and chiefly) because of the frozen ground. In summer the ground turns swampy over huge areas, and travel is very difficult. In winter the ground freezes rock hard and can be driven over by almost anything (snowmobiles, trucks, hovercraft, or anything else). What do you think are the best things to use in summer?

That's about it for an introduction to the character of the Arctic. You have a few points; let's summarize them. First is the lack of positive things; second the cold; third the lack of trees; fourth the drought and aridity; fifth the tundra vegetation; sixth the darkness; seventh the permafrost; eighth the lack of soil; ninth the hardness of the life for the people; tenth the low population densities; eleventh the remoteness; twelfth the vast distances inside the Arctic; thirteenth the lack of normal transportaion modes; and fourteenth the hazards of using even what transportation methods there are available.

And you were asked for only ten!

2 Energy

Before we go into detail with this topic, let us first of all realize that no one knows what energy is. All of us have a fair idea of what it does, what some of its effects look like, and we know that some forms of energy can be converted into others. But nobody yet knows what it *is.*

When we talk about energy as a resource, we don't mean energy pure and simple. Rather, we mean the various substances and forms that the energy our technology uses comes locked up in. As technology changes, so will the form of our energy sources. In the past we used to burn wood as a supplier of heat energy, candles for light energy, and that was about it. Today, we use coal, oil and natural gas, nuclear fuels, and only a little wood to supply ourselves with energy. Our technology has changed, and we are able to use forms of energy that our ancestors never had from energy resources that our ancestors did not perceive as being useful in that way.

By far the greatest amount of energy that Canadians use today is in the form of electricity. It is easy to transport over long distances with little or no loss due to friction or leakage. It can be converted into many other energy forms at the receiving end: light, heat, and motion, and can even be stored in the form of batteries, e.g., car batteries and lawnmower batteries. Without electricity, Canada would be uninhabitable during the winter and our industries would suffer great falls in production.

The fuel resources that we use to generate electricity would be useless without a certain amount of hardware — buildings, turbines, transmission lines, dams, furnaces, etc. In themselves, then, such man-made things can be counted as energy resources just as much as the fuels that they convert to our use. One would be useless without the other.

Province	installed capacity '000 kw		production million kwh	
	Hydro	Thermal	Hydro	Thermal
Newfoundland	972	279	4 653.4	167.8
Prince Edward I.	—	77	—	250.4
Nova Scotia	163	763	589.5	2 867.6
New Brunswick	563	630	2 656.9	2 461.4
Quebec	13 279	744	74 448.9	1 337.5
Ontario	6 797	6 819	39 092.5	24 741.9
Manitoba	1 319	472	7 768.7	665.4
Saskatchewan	586	952	2 610.1	3 378.4
Alberta	616	2 068	1 216.6	8 737.2
British Columbia	3 948	1 460	22 871.8	2 741.7
Yukon	26	21	180.7	39.9
North West Terr.	35	40	227.0	42.3
Canada total	28 304	14 325	156 316.1	47 431.5

Figure 2-1. 1970 energy statistics.

2-1. Construct two compound bars[2] to show Canada's 1970 electrical installed capacity by province. Line them up side by side on the same sheet of paper so that you can connect the upper and lower limits for each province by means of dotted lines. Comment on the absence of hydro from Prince Edward Island and the tremendous size of Quebec's hydro capacity. Confine your answers to geographical advantages and disadvantages.

Hydro power stations are usually installed where there is a large vertical drop in the course of a river. The potential and kinetic energy of the moving mass of water can be used to spin turbines connected to electrical generators. Often, the quantity of energy to be used can be increased by the construction of a dam to hold back the water and increase its depth. Besides increasing the *head of water* in this way, the dam also serves to regulate the flow of water so that unless exceptional weather conditions are experienced, the flow of water through the hydro power station remains fairly constant.

Naturally enough, Canada has exploited those sites for hydro power stations which are most accessible. There are still many more remaining but the cost of developing them is a little too high when the cost of generating electricity by thermal means is considered. Even so, a recent estimate of total unused hydro capacity on Canada's lakes and rivers runs as high as 60 million kw. The figure could be a good deal higher than this, though, because as technology develops, the means to make hydro power stations more efficient increases. Also, innovation could greatly raise the figure. If the Bay of Fundy, with tides in excess of 13 m and sometimes as high as 25 m, could be harnessed, then this would create a great deal of electric energy. The harnessing of the energy of several north-flowing rivers is planned at James Bay in the province of Quebec; installed capacity might reach 10 million kw by 1979.

The best places for Canada to generate hydro power are where the rivers of the Canadian Shield flow off this glaciated area into the lower land that flanks it. Happily, these sites are found on the north side of the St. Lawrence valley lowlands — just where the greatest numbers of Canada's people and industries are to be found. One of the first hydro power stations built in Canada is at Niagara Falls. The Sir Adam Beck station uses its power during the off-peak periods (when would that be?) to pump water back up to a reservoir behind it. This can be used to turn generators during the peak periods when most electricity is required.

2-2. What season of the year do you think demands the generation of most electrical power? Why? Would it be easy for hydro stations to produce power during that season? Give reasons for your answer.

2-3. Using the production data for electricity in the provinces to be found in Figure 2-1, decide which is the cheaper way of producing electricity. Is it by hydro means or by thermal means? Describe the method you used to find out the answer.

Thermal power stations burn oil, coal, and natural gas to turn the turbines which are connected to the generators. The burning fuel heats water into steam which emerges onto the turbine blades under high pressure. Some cities in Canada are experimenting with burning trash as a means of generat-

The Athabasca Tar Sands. This outcrop lies along the Athabasca River, northern Alberta. About 8 to 10 m thick, the Tar Sands cover vast areas and constitute an immense store of energy.

ing electricity. They have to burn it anyway, so why not make a profit out of it? In 1969 Canada burned 11 873 750 tonnes of coal, 92 730 990 litres of fuel oil, and 450 856 000 000 cubic m of natural gas to produce electricity.

Something you are probably aware of is that Canada has quite large reserves of petroleum (oil and natural gas.) By far the greatest proportion of these reserves is found in Alberta, where the 1970 proven reserves totalled some 89 percent of all Canada's. Since then, part of the Athabasca Tar Sands have been counted in so that Alberta holds well over 90 percent of Canada's crude petroleum reserves. Proven reserves only tell us part of the story though. In 1970 Canada had proven reserves of 1 150 million tonnes of petroleum. An undisclosed amount of oil existed over and above that, its existence being merely guessed at, or kept secret for a variety of reasons, or able to become available only as technology improves. This is where the Tar Sands come in. Even though only some parts of this resource can be said to be economically exploitable by today's technology and at today's prices, this small proportion multiplies by a factor of three the crude oil reserves of Canada and extends production at present levels from 15 to 62 years.

Province	production (percent)	
	crude oil	natural gas
New Brunswick	0.002	0.006
Ontario	0.2	0.007
Manitoba	1.4	0.8
Saskatchewan	19.7	2.8
Alberta	72.7	82.4
British Columbia	5.8	14.0
North West Terr.	0.02	0.001

Note: totals may not equal 100% due to rounding.

Figure 2-2. Petroleum production in Canada, 1970.

> 2-4. Construct two divided circles[5] to show the sources of production of crude oil in 1970 and natural gas in 1970.

At the moment Canada is conducting exploration of the Arctic and its continental shelves in order to decide if there is oil there or not. The Pan Arctic Oils Company is composed of 20 oil companies and the Canadian government, which holds 45 percent of the shares. So far it has spent well over $50 million to strike petroleum fields in Melville Island and King Christian Island. Shell Canada is active off the coast of Nova Scotia, where the federal government has divided the seafloor into concession blocks that oil companies bid for. So far Shell has struck oil off Sable Island.

One thing that characterizes the operations of the oil companies is secrecy. When they are drilling wells that cost perhaps $10 million each at sea, they are naturally very reluctant to disclose whether or not they have struck oil for fear that this would affect the bidding for the right to drill in adjacent concessions.

The oil in western Canada is gathered together via pipelines at Edmonton. From Edmonton a large pipeline crosses the Rockies to Vancouver and another snakes east underground to finish up in southern Ontario. East of the Ottawa valley, oil is imported. Why would that be?

Origin	Destination	kilometres	Tariff per unit volume
Edmonton	Vancouver	1 150	40.0 cents
	Regina	700	20.7
	Winnipeg	1 355	32.7
	Sarnia	2 790	48.0
	Port Credit	3 040	51.0
Portland (U.S.)	Montreal	380	11.0

Figure 2-3. Oil tariffs for Canadian cities, 1970.

> 2-5. Figure 2-3 shows you how much it costs to ship oil to various Canadian cities by pipeline from various sources. Remember, Montreal is east of the Ottawa valley and so it receives its oil from abroad through tankers which unload at Portland, Maine, U.S.A. We can assume that pipeline technology is the same all over North America so that the operating costs of any pipeline are about the same unless special factors are encountered when the pipeline is built.
>
> Plot the data as a single line graph. Five of the points you will be able to join with a smooth curve. If it had been a straight line it would have meant that oil pipeline tariffs increase at a steady rate. However, it is a curve. What does that mean? Why? Which city is not on the curve? Why not?

Of all the electricity used in Canada in 1970, industry took 58 percent. The mining industry used 22 percent, pulp and paper took another 15 percent, and chemicals and iron and steel took another 10 percent. Other industries used 11 percent. Domestic use of electricity for heating, lighting, and cooking as well as the operation of various appliances took 20 percent. The commercial use of electricity for telephones, neon signs, shop lighting, etc., took another 13 percent. That left 9 percent lost or unaccounted for.

2-6. Construct a percentage bar graph[3] to show the uses of electricity in Canada in 1970. How do you account for the missing 9 percent?

Well, the energy crisis is with us or so we are told. Oil is becoming more costly and natural gas more difficult to find. In addition the conflict between Arab and Jew in the Middle East, the richest oil area in the world, means that eastern Canada's oil supplies might become problematical. Finally, it could be said that refinery capacity in Canada is too low so that even if the crude oil was available, not enough gasoline or heating oil, as well as all the other petroleum products, could be produced.

As a solution to a problem well illustrated by Venezuela raising its price of crude oil to $7 per barrel in 1973, it is proposed to continue the trans-Canada pipeline to the east so that Canada does not have to depend on supplies from abroad. Anything to be free of OPEC!

Shell Canada

Sedneth I drilling vessel, drilling off the east coast of Canada. The standby vessel is in the foreground. September 1970.

Domestic oil refined per day	55 percent
Foreign oil refined per day	45 percent

Crude oil imports — barrels refined per day

*Venezuela	364 000
*Iran	55 000
*Nigeria	48 000
*Saudi Arabia	29 000
*Iraq	23 000
Colombia	20 000
*Union of Arab Emirates	14 000
*Kuwait	13 000
*Trinidad	6 000

*Organisation of Petroleum Exporting Countries (OPEC)

Figure 2-4.   Daily refinery statistics Canada, 1970.

2-7.   Use the data in Figure 2-4 to construct a divided circle[5] to show the amount of oil that is refined daily in Canada from domestic sources and from the total of foreign sources. Cut your circle into the two sectors that you have drawn and, on a map of Canada, stick the domestic sector west of the Ottawa valley and the foreign sector east of the Ottawa valley. (Or you can draw the sectors directly if you wish.)

Use the rest of the data in Figure 2-4 to construct proportional arrows[11] showing the origin of Canada's oil imports as well as the quantities refined per day. On the west side of the Ottawa valley, draw a proportional arrow to represent the domestic oil refined each day. If the oil refinery capacity of Canada in 1970 was 135 units per day and 127 units was actually refined, what percentage of daily capacity was utilized? That does not leave much of a margin, does it?

Apart from oil, another fossil fuel that is receiving greater attention now than it has for decades is coal. Originally, Canada's coal reserves were exploited for powering railway engines, for burning as a house fuel, for use as coke in steel production, and a few other things. With the advent of oil, coal production dropped but it did not die out. In recent years the greater demand for electricity has resulted in more coal-burning power stations being built and so the demand for Canadian coal has risen. Today, some five provinces produce coal. In 1970 Canada produced 16 604 164 tonnes of coal. Alberta, Saskatchewan, and British Columbia produced 85 percent of this. Mostly using it for the thermal generation of electricity, the Japanese bought 4 400 000 tonnes of Canadian coal, mainly from the western provinces, in 1970. Ontario actually imported coal for this purpose from the U.S. In 1970 the province imported 189 000 tonnes of coal for thermal power stations and the iron and steel industry. It was cheaper to import it from Pittsburgh rather than use Canadian coal because the transport costs would have been too high.

For the future, it is not yet certain how prominent nuclear power stations like the Pickering, Ontario, station will be. Radioactive waste disposal poses some problems and at the moment, the cost per unit of power is higher than from conventional sources. How long that will last is anyone's guess. The CANDU reactor system uses Canadian uranium that has also been processed here. Although it uses heavy water instead of ordinary water for cooling, this reactor system has a good foreign sales potential. Even now we use some power from nuclear power stations, and when one considers that in 1951 hydro power was 90 percent of total electrical production but only 66 percent in 1971 then the quest for alternative sources of power becomes a necessity.

3 Farming Settlement Patterns

AREAL DIFFERENTIATION

The first farming in Canada is attributed to the Huron Indians of south Ontario. They cleared parts of the forest by burning, after cutting the trees down to within a metre of the ground. Hard work for people in the Stone Age! It took many years before enough land was cleared in order to farm it. The forest belonged to everyone, and anybody could clear as much as desired.

The Hurons preferred village sites above steep slopes as a defence precaution. Other requirements were fertile sandy soils for agriculture and a good supply of fresh water. Tilling the soil with digging sticks, the Hurons grew corn, beans, cucumber, squash, melons and a little tobacco. Since crop rotation and fertilizing were almost unknown except by accident, every ten or twelve years a village site would be abandoned and the population would move to a newly cleared site on which work had begun perhaps four years before. After 1650 the forest took over these sites completely. The Hurons had been decimated by Iroquois attack and disease brought by Europeans. The land they had occupied was not cleared again until the early nineteenth century.

Elsewhere in Canada the native peoples survived by hunting animals and gathering nuts, roots, and berries. They were not nearly as settled as the Hurons, since they had to follow their food supplies. As a rule, we can say that the land of Canada was not settled permanently until the advent of the Europeans.

The first permanent settlements in Canada were French. French settlement was a reflection of French feudal society in Europe. A land grant of as much as 3 000 sq. km would be made to a *seigneur*. The land would be raw, covered in forest which would have to be removed for farming. Instead of the impossible task of clearing all the land by himself, the seigneur would divide it into lots or *rotures*. These lots he would grant free to a settler or *habitant* who would undertake to pay a nominal tax to the seigneur in return for being allowed to work it. Along the St. Lawrence River were established some 240 seigneuries occupying some 3.2 million hectares.

The *rang* system of settlement was devised by the seigneurs. They divided their holdings as seen in Figure 3-1. Each row of lots was called a rang and fronted a river or a road (a communication route.) There were several advantages to this system:

   i) a man could live on his own land and support himself and his family.

   ii) neighbours were always close at hand.

   iii) a transportation route was always very close.

   iv) the lots were easily surveyed.

   v) the land was fairly divided. From the meadow lands along the river

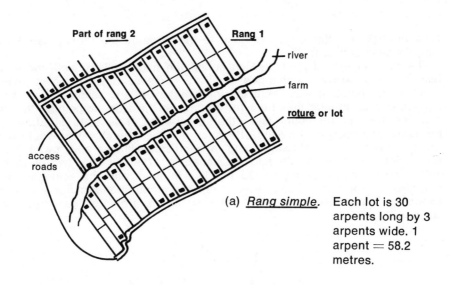

Part of rang 2   Rang 1

river

farm

roture or lot

access
roads

(a) *Rang simple*. Each lot is 30 arpents long by 3 arpents wide. 1 arpent = 58.2 metres.

(b) *Rang double*.   5 *rangs doubles* = 1 *canton* (township)

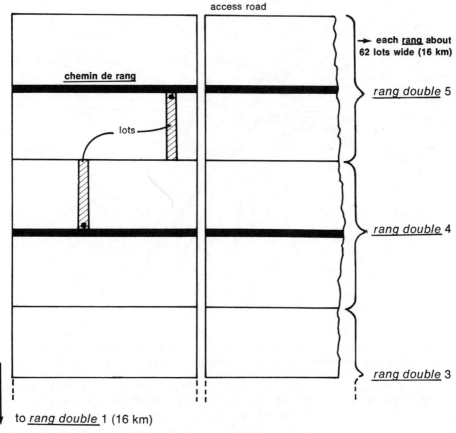

access road

→ each rang about 62 lots wide (16 km)

chemin de rang

rang double 5

lots

rang double 4

rang double 3

to *rang double* 1 (16 km)

Figure 3-1.   French settlement patterns.

15

bank through the cleared lands back to the woodlot, the farmer had a wide range of soil conditions.

The rang system of land division suited the habitant very well. Its pattern has survived largely unchanged until the present day. It meant that in practice the habitant was relatively independent of his seigneur and it was not difficult to indulge in a little fur-trading on the side, something that was reserved for the seigneurs and other dignitaries. This state of affairs did not commend itself to the King of France nor the Church. They would much rather have had the habitants living in nucleated villages and towns. Six of these were laid out by the fall of Quebec in 1759 but only two were ever built. The habitants simply would not live in them and the seigneurs were powerless to force them. Land was cheap and plentiful and labour scarce and expensive. Who would willingly take a lot (roture) from an oppressive seigneur?

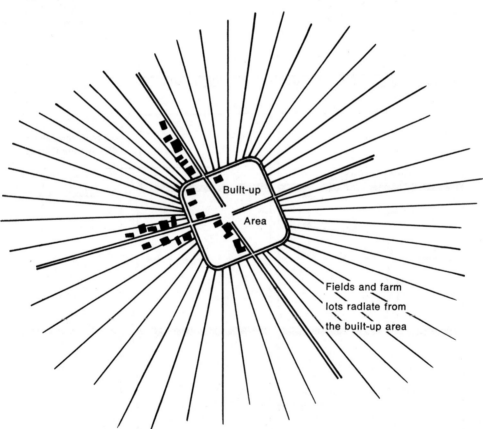

Figure 3-2. The radial system. Designed by Jean Talon, first Intendant of Nouvelle France. This type of nucleated settlement was not popular with the *habitants*.

As time marched on and the profit margin in farming shrank, many tenants gave up their lots and they reverted to woodland. As the pressure for farmers to work larger and larger holdings was increased by the force

Department of Energy, Mines and Resources, Ottawa

Figure 3-3.

17

of economic circumstance, some weaknesses of the rang system were apparent. The farm buildings were poorly sited on the lot and farmers spent a great deal of their time simply walking. Also, the rangs and lots had been laid out on a map. The boundaries often cut straight across lakes, marshes and peat bogs. They took no account of things like soil fertility.

Away from the St. Lawrence the land to the south as far as the U.S. border was surveyed in Quebec by the British. They did not use the rang system in these Eastern Townships, as they came to be called. Starting at the end of the eighteenth century, townships 16 km square were laid out. On water frontage, a rectangular township with sides of 14.4 km and 19.2 km was used. The narrow edge fronted the water. Each township contained 10 concessions and each concession contained 28 lots. The concessions ran parallel to the river. Lot sizes were about 81 hectares, once allowances for roads and a town site had been made, and were much closer to squares than the rang lots.

3-1. On graph paper, and using a suitable scale, construct proportional rectangles to show the areas in

i) a rang simple lot

ii) a rang double lot

iii) an Eastern Township lot.

Insert your rectangles inside each other so that at least two sides are common. For example:

3-2. What system of land division is shown in Figure 3-3? Back up what you say by placing tracing paper over the map and picking out all the relevant features that helped you to make your decision.

If you are really sharp-eyed, you will be able to put on some of the lots and rangs.

Farther west than Quebec (Lower Canada) lay Ontario (Upper Canada). Land settlement here was very different from the way it had gone on in Quebec. There was a great deal of experimentation with townships in various sizes. Square townships ultimately resulted with sides ranging from 9.6 km to 16 km in length. The basic unit of the Ontario township was the block of 12 lots.

18

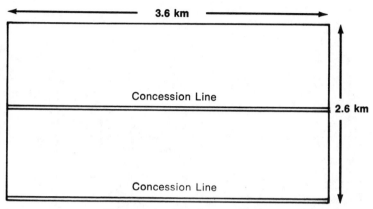

Figure 3-4.   The Ontario Block.

The block was six lots wide and two deep. By 1829 enough confusion had resulted for the provincial government to pass a law standardizing the township surveys. The dimensions of the lots and blocks were fixed as shown in Figure 3-4 but some odd-shaped townships resulted.

The reason for this was that the early settlers came in by boat and disembarked on the shores of Lake Ontario. They would lay a base line parallel to the water's edge and then proceed to survey concession lines parallel with this base line. Side roads every two lots cut across at right angles. Since townships were often begun independently of each other, there was often confusion when townships met each other.

3-3.   On assignment 3-1, insert a similar rectangle, drawn to scale, of the standardized Ontario lot.

3-4.   Lay a sheet of tracing paper on the map extract of St. Catharines to be found in Figure 3-5. The concessions, as you can see, are numbered in Roman numerals. Mark in the concession lines and the roads running inland from Lake Ontario. Pencil in the shoreline of Lake Ontario but not the Welland canal. Detach your tracing and set to work to restore the original lot pattern. Number your lots from right to left as you face the lake. Compare the original lot pattern with the present-day use of the land. What covers lots 1-4 on concessions V and VI today? What else has been superimposed on the original lot pattern?

If you measure the size of each lot you will find it smaller than the law of 1829 said it should be. Can you suggest why this might be so?

It was on the prairies that the gridiron pattern of surveying reached perfection (or near perfection.) Early explorers came back with accounts of a flat (at least in the east) plain with few trees to obscure the line-of-sight, covered with tall grasses and buffalo. The buffalo had been all but wiped out in five years of systematic butchery prior to 1880. The land was now open to settlers who might come in by train and break the tough, tall-grass sod with steel ploughs to plant wheat which would be exported to a hungry Europe.

The advantages of the prairie system of townships were many. A settler

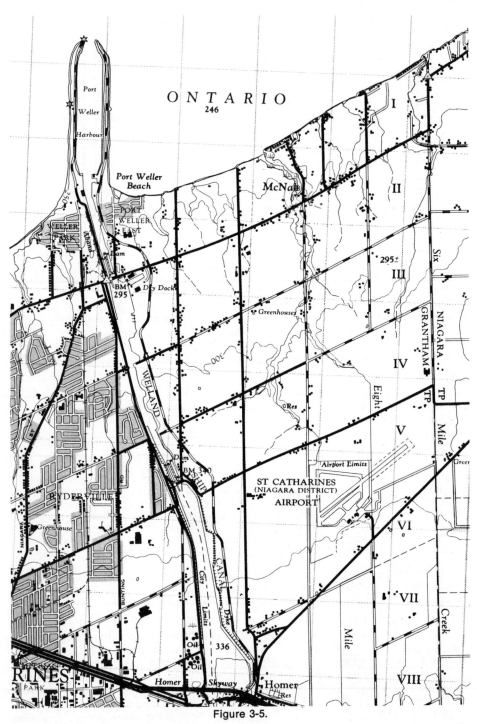

Figure 3-5.

Department of Energy, Mines and Resources, Ottawa

could easily find his own land — even pick out the section he wanted from a map. The fact that the land was fairly flat allowed for easy surveying and marking. In addition the square township pattern could be extended indefinitely to cover just as much land as was required. In fact, several hundred townships were laid out and not all the land in them was ever claimed.

Lt.-Governor Archibald of Manitoba imported the American township plan in 1869 in order to divide up the prairies. The township would be square with the length of one side being 9.6 km. Divided into 36 sections, each section was further subdivided into square quarter-sections measuring 0.8 km along each side. The area of each quarter-section was about 64 hectares. This would be the homesteading unit unless a town was laid out, in which case a section would be cut into 16 subdivisions (squares again). The area of a subdivision was about 16 hectares.

Access was important, of course. It was provided that north-south roads would run between every section, east-west roads would run between every pair of sections.

3-5.   Draw a diagram of a prairie township. Put in the section numbers. Here is a clue. The numbers on the east side of the township running north to south are 36, 25, 24, 13, 12, 1.

If the townships were aligned with lines of longitude, what problem would be encountered as the survey proceeded north?

As the settlers swarmed onto the prairies after 1885, they found about half the land was available for settlement. To encourage the railway companies to build a line, the federal government had allowed them every odd-numbered section in every township. In addition, the Hudson's Bay Company had lost the chance to continue exploiting the land which had included some of the prairies. They were allowed section 8 and the majority of section 26 (all of it save for the north-east quarter section. On every fifth township they were granted all of section 26.) Finally, school sections 11 and 29 were to be sold at auction to provide the money for a school building.

3-6.   On the map that you drew for assignment 3-5, use colours and a legend to show the railway grants, the school lands, and the lands granted to the HBC as compensation. (This is a fourth township.)

If the HBC received 10 million hectares of land in this way, how many townships were planned? How much land did the railway companies receive?

Today, most of these railway lands and those of the HBC have been sold. Pretty well all the prairies are now farmed but there is still some homesteading in the northern prairies.

Not quite all of the prairies were settled in this manner, however. In 1812 an agricultural settlement had been made along the Red River which flows north into Lake Winnipeg. The man in charge was Lord Selkirk of the Hudson's Bay Company, and he received the land grant from them. The settlers were Scots, removed from their ancestral homes by the Highland clearances. Although they had a rough beginning with plagues of "hoppers" as well as epidemics and floods, they survived. Each settler had a lot of some 40.5

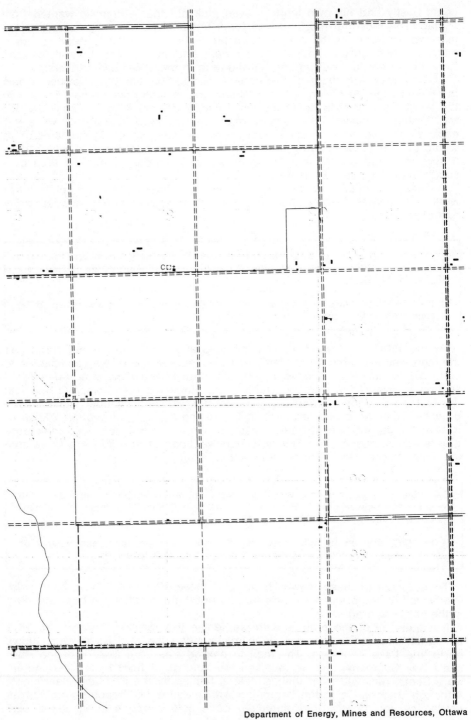

Department of Energy, Mines and Resources, Ottawa

Figure 3-6.

hectares with 1.6 hectares fronting the Red River. What settlement pattern does that remind you of?

It was to avoid this most un-American system of land division that the first prairie townships were measured west of a longitude line about 50 km west of the Red River. Northwards, they extended as far as the 60th parallel.

As noted earlier, settlers swarmed into the prairies once they had been made accessible by rail. By the start of the First World War, nearly two million of them had settled there. Since that time the prairies have declined in population. The hungry years of the Depression and the over-reliance on one crop spelled disaster when the dry years of the early 1930s began. People left their land, selling to neighbours who thus increased their holdings. They had to enlarge their farms in order to continue profitably.

Overall on the prairies, there is a clear link between the density of farm settlement and the size of a farm, along with the fertility and moisture in its soil. The most fertile black earths of the central south prairies generally have four farms per section (the original planned density). North of the black earths only one-third of the farms in any township are of a quarter section. The rest are larger, maybe one-half to whole sections in size. In the drier west, ranching country, farms (ranches) may be several sections in size

---

3-7. Lay a sheet of tracing paper over the map in Figure 3-6. For one township only, divide it into sections and put on the farms. These are a small black rectangle (farmhouse) and a larger black rectangle (the barn). What is the average size of a farm in terms of sections? Is this land very fertile — a black earth perhaps?

Land settlement, once begun, is fixed, often for long periods of time. It stamps a country's surface with its history. Even if a small village becomes a town or city, the original pattern of the streets is usually discernible to some extent. In the case of Canada, the diversity of its land settlement patterns is a living book. The story it tells should be known to every Canadian. It is part of the Canadian heritage.

4 The Fishing Industry

CONSTANT CHANGE

Consider these facts:
- The coastline of Canada is more than 50 000 km in length.
- Marine waters are shallow and of trawling depth. They are also plankton-rich, partly because of the mixing of the waters of two ocean currents off the east coast.
- Most of Canada's fishing grounds back onto coasts furnished with many fine natural harbours ideally suited to fishing boats.
- Inland lakes and waters cover at least 750 000 square km.
- There are at least 150 commercially exploited fish species in Canadian waters. Still others exist in commercial quantities but have not yet been developed, e.g., the capelin.

With all Canada's natural advantages, it is no surprise to find that Canada has always had a strong, profitable fishing industry. Many Indians and Eskimos had fish as a staple item in their diets before John Cabot arrived on the Grand Banks in 1497. He reported that his sailors could catch cod simply by lowering baskets on ropes into the sea. He further intimated that a flung spear could not penetrate the water for the press of fish and that he could have walked to shore dryshod across their backs.

Whether or not you believe such fishy stories, it is true that before the mainland of Canada was graced with permanent European settlements, its offshore waters on the east coast saw fleets of English, French, Spanish, and Portuguese vessels come to reap Nature's finned bounty. Usually there was little or no competition, but once in a while the consequences of a European war were felt here; fishing stations on sheltered coves established to dry and cure the cod would be attacked and destroyed by the agents of belligerent powers.

Even with the occasional threat of war, fishing perhaps 5 000 km away from home was still profitable. Primitive meat preserving techniques made salt cod a luxury in England. It sold for more than ten times the price of fresh beef at perhaps $8.00 for 50 kg. Of course, that was during the early sixteenth century!

In the early days of the cod fishery, the cod was simply salted. Later on, a new system called "flaking" came into being. The cod was split open and dried on racks called flakes. Less salt was needed to complete the cure and the dried cod occupied less volume.

The salt cod trade with the West Indies in the late seventeenth and eighteenth centuries gave Canada in return rum, sugar, and molasses. After its peak in the 1880s, the salt cod trade declined following the introduction of refrigeration. This decline continues until the present day but is likely never to die out completely.

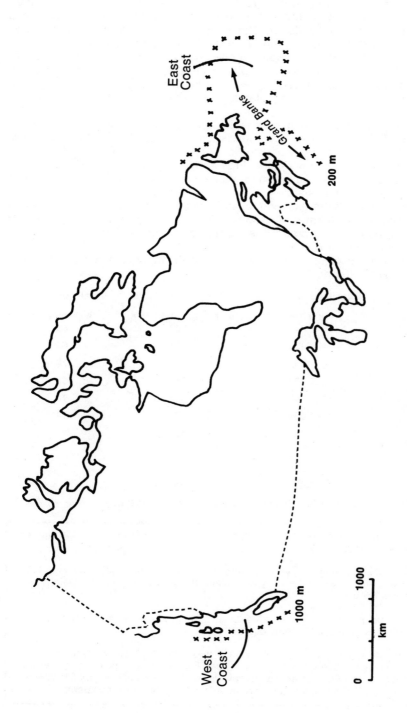

Figure 4-1. Canada and her marine fishing grounds. The territorial limit is too close to the coast to be shown on this scale.

East Coast

Grand Banks

200 m

1000 m

West Coast

1000

km

0

In 1908 the otter trawler or dragger came into use. In 1923 came the filleting and quick freezing of the catch. In 1963 the precooked, breaded, and frozen fish stick made its debut. The days of schooners and dories which handlined for cod were numbered. Trawlers now took their catch to modern processing plants. Even the plants themselves became larger and more efficient. In 1920 there were only 53 plants on the east coast which had in excess of a $50 000 processed value. By 1960 there were 296 although the total number of fish processing plants had declined from a 1920 figure of 571 to 478.

The story of fishing on Canada's west coast dates mainly from 1885 when the transcontinental railway was constructed. In 1840, the first fish was caught and canned on the west coast. It was not until 1869 that the first salmon cannery was set up on the Fraser river. Today the industry is concentrated around Prince Rupert and Vancouver. Next to salmon, halibut is the second most valuable species.

Today on Canada's coasts and inland waters, the most modern gear is used. Echo sounders locate fish shoals; power machinery takes in nets and may process the catch on board. Electronic navigation equipment is commonplace and every ship carries a radio.

Let us look more closely at the industry itself, though, and try to discern some of the recent trends.

	Total landed weight ('000 tonnes)	Value of all products of the fisheries ($m.)	Total number of fishermen ('000)
1950	1 048	153	65
1955	965	181	63
1960	935	198	78
1965	1 262	310	80
1966	1 346	358	73
1967	1 259	330	71
1968	1 452	390	72
1969	1 351	390	63
1970	1 336	427	62
1971	1 000	463	59

Figure 4-2. Selected Canadian fishery statistics.

4-1. Calculate index numbers[6] for the data in Figure 4-2 using the 1950 figures as a base of 100 in each case.

Construct a multiple-line, time-series graph[8] to show your index numbers. Take care with the time scale! How do you explain an increased catch by weight and value with fewer fishermen?

How can it be possible for the value of all fish products to more than double if the weight has increased by only one half?

If the value of a fisherman's catch in 1950 was almost $2 354.00, what was the value of each fisherman's catch in each year for which you have data? Set out your answers in the form of an additional line on your graph and label it "fisherman productivity." Remember, your graph is plotted with index numbers!

Now you have a clearer idea of recent trends in the Canadian fishing industry. If your impression so far is that production has peaked or reached a plateau, then you might be right. There are all kinds of reasons why the Canadian fishing industry faces problems. Competition from foreign fishing vessels which operate in international waters off all coasts where fish spawn in the shallow, nutrient-rich water has lowered fish stocks to the point where the survival of several species is in question. There will probably always be fish, of course, but whether they will continue to exist in commercial quantities is another matter.

Canada's east coast fisheries feel the pinch worst. Although the Canadian territorial waters extend 18 km, to further extend this protection to 320 km is necessary if the spawning grounds of the Grand Banks are to be protected. In June 1973, the federal government agreed that the limit should be 320 km but decided to wait until the "Law of the Sea" conference should meet in 1974.

All told, Canada is party to ten international fishing agreements and conventions, yet there is still no generally accepted plan to decide on annual allowable catches for each species. What is everyone's property becomes no one's responsibility. When Canada does extend her protection to the Grand Banks, it will not be detrimental to any country's long-term interests. Other countries will still be able to fish there but on a regulated, controlled basis. As you will soon find out, this is vitally necessary.

	Canada	U.S.	U.S.S.R.	Total
1964	57.4	60.4	12.9	141.1
1965	50.4	60.7	128.8	248.8
1966	61.5	60.0	73.5	203.6
1967	56.0	44.7	8.4	117.3
1968	49.6	32.0	3.2	96.7
1969	44.3	20.8	0.3	72.3
1970	26.9	12.2	0.9	48.0
1971	29.2	9.8	1.4	47.1

Figure 4-3.   North West Atlantic haddock catch in thousands of tonnes.

4-2.   Construct a multiple-line, time-series graph[8] to show the data in Figure 4-3. Which country had an abnormally high catch of haddock in 1965? What happened to the total catch in succeeding years? What do you think about the situation? What would you do to improve it?

There is a disquieting trend to Canada's fish catches in recent years. The catches for several important species have been declining. The conclusion is that a narrow coastal fishing zone of 18 km is not enough. Spawning grounds have to be included if the survival of commercial fishing for several species is to be assured.

	(a) Saltwater species				(b) Freshwater species		
	East coast cod	East coast herring	East coast lobster	West coast salmon	White-fish	Yellow Pickerel	Blue Pickerel
1950	113	105	20	84	11	6	9
1955	263	90	22	59	10	9	12
1960	274	110	23	34	12	6	5 tonnes
1965	261	184	18	41	11	4	—
1966	255	249	17	74	9	5	—
1967	237	346	16	60	8	4	—
1968	269	524	17	80	8	4	—
1969	245	487	18	36	9	4	—
1970	219	470	17	69	9	3	—
1971	204	419	17	60	8	3	—

Figure 4-4. Domestic catches of some significant fish species in Canada. All figures rounded to nearest '000 tonnes.

4-3. Construct two multiple-line, time-series graphs[8] to show the data in Figure 4-4(a) and 4-4 (b).

Looking at the lines for east coast herring and cod, suggest why they show a sharp decline after the late 1960s.

Freshwater catches are also down. Why?

If the picture painted so far is too gloomy for you to take, don't despair. After all, when you think about it, fishing, for all its sophisticated gear, is still in a primitive hunting stage. Wouldn't it be much easier to farm and harvest fish, much as we do land animals like cows and sheep and hogs?

Fish farming is actually practised in Canada today. An eel farm was established on the Pokemouche River, New Brunswick. Fresh, frozen, and smoked two-year-old eels are exported to Europe and Japan, where prices reach $9.00 a kg.

Nova Scotia has the Fisheries Research Board at Halifax which has produced large lobsters cultured artificially (artifishally?) by altering the balance of their hormones. In addition, it has been found that although a wild lobster may take at least three to six years to reach a harvestable size, if lobsters are grown in calm tanks and subjected to the minimum of interference while the temperature of the water is maintained at 21°C or a little above, then harvestable sizes are attained in less than a year. Feed is cheap, and the wastage rate in the wild of perhaps 999 lobsters out of 1 000 eaten by predators before adulthood is eliminated.

Trout farming in prairie sloughs and ponds has met with great success.

Trout and salmon hatcheries supply fingerlings to stock lakes and ponds for the sport fisherman. On the whole though, fish farming is in its infancy in Canada.

Canada's short-term fishing interests will be better served by continuing to work internationally for quotas in order to preserve fish stocks. This policy had some success in 1972. The International Commission on North Atlantic Fisheries' 15 members all agreed to quotas thereby limiting their catches that year. ICNAF experts also concluded that the North Atlantic fishing fleets should be reduced by 50 percent to assure the industry of a future. At the moment that seems unlikely.

In 1971, foreign fishing fleets took 1.2 million tonnes of fish off Canada's coasts while Canada took 1 million tonnes.

You already know the story of the Atlantic haddock. It is similar to the tale of the west coast herring which had become so scarce by 1968 that all fishing for it was ordered suspended by the Ottawa government for three years. A limited take of 105 000 tonnes was permitted in 1972. This kind of action would greatly benefit the east coast salmon. For centuries no one knew where the salmon spent its adult life at sea until the Danes discovered its feeding ranges off the Greenland eastern coast. They continue to net the salmon in their territorial waters despite pleas from all Atlantic seaboard countries with salmon streams. They have agreed to phase out netting by 1975 but by then it will likely be too late, at least for commercial fishing. Too few adults will be left to return to individual streams and spawn.

The west coast of Canada is most fortunate in that the territorial limit of 18 km is effectively extended many more kilometres than this by the numerous islands along the coast. Spawning grounds along the coast are largely protected and recovery programs like that instituted for the herring will prove effective.

Above all, though, the foreign fishing fleets of Russia, East Germany, and Poland must be regulated. Japan is also a menace in this respect of overfishing. Gang fishing by great factory ships, each of which carries up to 14 trawlers, has already scoured the ocean bed of many of the Atlantic banks areas. Pretty well everything that swims is taken. Electric charges stun the shoals and gigantic pumps suck the helpless creatures aboard for processing.

All this despite an estimate that the world's oceans could yield a sustainable annual catch of twice the present figure if only quotas and minimum taking sizes could be agreed upon and enforced.

As a final insight into the growth of Canada's fishing industry and as a reminder that it would be tragic were it ever to decline because of a lack of co-operation at a variety of levels, examine Figure 4-5.

	West coast		Inland		East coast	
1919	15.2	(0.4)	4.2	(0.2)	18.5	(0.4)
1969	47.3	(0.7)	15.5	(0.4)	115.5	(1.3)

Figure 4-5. The growth of Canada's fishing industry. Catches are shown as value landed with s.r. numbers in brackets.

4-4. Trace an outline map of Canada from Figure 4-1 and locate concentric, proportional circles[4] upon it to illustrate the data in Figure 4-5.

The future of Canada's fishing industry will be determined by progress made during the 1970s. Satellites even now can track schools and direct fleets to intercept them. Scientists travelling with fleets can interpret signs and clues so that the taking up of shoals of fish will become even more effective. The ocean is not an unlimited reservoir of food. It is susceptible to pollution and abuse. It would be tragic if commercial fishing were to be curtailed or eliminated due to international short-sightedness.

5 Foreign Aid

GLOBAL VIEW

A tractor followed by shrieking small children raises a cloud of red dust in a Nigerian village. Hybrid wheat lies dormant in a Colombian storehouse, waiting for the most opportune time to be planted. A bank official in Toronto sticks down the flap of an envelope. The enclosed letter authorizes a credit transfer to the account of a Canadian executive in Kenya. Wheat elevators thrust into the silent prairie sky, brooding over crawling combines and totally unaware that their contents will eventually be crammed into the mouths of famine victims in Bihar state, India. Canadian water flows south. A Parry Sound teacher sits marking papers beneath an oriental print while a gently turning fan on the ceiling disturbs Brunei's sultry air. A Ghanaian student on the campus of the Western University, London, Ontario, is munching a lunchtime hamburger and reflecting that it doesn't compare with kola nut stew.

What you have just read are fine threads in a net which binds together Canada and many overseas countries. But the net is invisible. It has its existence in the hearts and minds of men of many different colours, cultures, and creeds. Along its strands flow money, men, ideas, and technology. The net is otherwise known as Canadian aid to other countries — foreign aid.

Aid categories $ millions

	Bilateral	Multilateral	Private	Total
Canada total aid	286	94	177	557
Canadian aid as a percentage of the world total				4
Canadian aid coefficient				6.8
World total aid	6 264	1 048	6 062	13 734

Figure 5-1. Canadian aid in perspective, 1971.

Now, just what is foreign aid? Many people have the mistaken impression that it is in the form of a gift. In fact, very little of Canada's foreign aid is in the form of a gift, and neither is that of many other countries. Rather, the aid is in the form of export credits, loans, and people.

Export credits. If a country wants to import something from Canada (wheat or tractors, for example), it has to pay in Canadian dollars. But it is not easy for a poor country to have that many Canadian dollars so Canada lets the poor countries have the exports on credit. When the poor countries finally save enough Canadian dollars, they pay their bills. Export credits are usually for things that a country needs from Canada in a hurry.

Credits outstanding on December 31	Wheat	Total
1965	293	586
1966	401	627
1967	273	520
1968	201	491
1969	187	503
1970	242	632
1971	360	862

Figure 5-2. Canadian export credits (millions $).

5-2. Construct a multiple-line graph[6] to show the data in Figure 5-2. Shade everything under the wheat line in yellow and everything between the wheat line and the total line in red. Call the red area "other export credits." What sort of things go into that category? See if you can tell why the line for wheat goes up steeply on your graph for the late 1960s and the early 1970s.

Loans. Generally loans are for long-term development projects in poor countries, the kind of projects that will help a country to help itself. What kind of projects might they be?

Two kinds of loan are made. Canada either lends directly to another country or to an international investment agency. The first kind of loan is a bilateral loan. It is interest-free and can be paid back over as long as 50 years, with the first payment taking place 10 years after the loan was made. The second kind of loan, to international development agencies, has interest rates of up to 7¾%. Even these are sometimes interest-free.

Loans made in the year	Bilateral loans			Loans made to international development agencies
	Latin America and the Caribbean	Asia	Africa	
1966	2	8	1	24
1967	3	17	2	16
1968	8	38	2	30
1969	8	48	3	30
1970	12	92	8	32
1971	13	93	33	53

all figures in million $

Figure 5-3.   Loans made by the Canadian government.

5-3.   Total the bilateral loans for each year and plot your totals as one line on a time series graph.[6] Plot the loans made to international development agencies as another line on the same graph. What trend can you see?

People. In 1971, Canada sent 241 technical advisers and 855 educators to developing countries and took in 1 832 students from those countries to study at Canadian universities and colleges.

Generally a country receiving Canadian aid is best off to have a mixed program. Export credits supply immediate needs while loans for projects and technical personnel to advise build up the kinds of things that a country needs for its long-term development. These might include power stations, irrigation and flood-control schemes, and mineral development.

Canada has many agencies to allocate its aid funds. The Canadian International Development Agency is Canada's oldest. It was begun in 1951 to help newly emerging south and south-east Asian countries. By 1962, aid was also going to Africa, the Caribbean and Latin America, and various countries in the Commonwealth. Altogether aid goes to more than 70 countries from CIDA. Whereas in 1963-1964 CIDA made $64.4 million available, by 1971-1972 this figure had grown to $426.4 million.

The Export Development Corporation lends foreign countries the money they need to buy Canadian goods. While the terms of the loans are very easy, as noted before, there has been criticism that because these loans are only to be used to buy Canadian goods, this aid benefits Canada as much as it does the recipient. In effect, Canada has extended its export market while the country which has borrowed money for machinery is not allowed to buy that machinery in the world markets at the cheapest price. However, Canada is not alone in this. Most other countries which give aid will give only "tied loans." It is not too difficult to see why tied loans aren't very popular with some people. Can you see why the Canadian government might insist on it, though?

While Canadian *government* money is invested and spent abroad, there are several *non-government* agencies, some of them subsidized by CIDA, which also give money but far more importantly, volunteer workers—thousands of them.

The Canadian Executive Service Overseas sends volunteers in the field of management and administration overseas to help in the setting up of new industry and government services.

We know how
to use your know-how

James Green, Barbados

Captain C. Boyd Shannon, Brazil

Fred A. Beeby, India

Gaston Hérald, Philippines

Canadian Executive Service Overseas

The Canadian University Service Overseas sent 1 300 graduates to 44 countries in 1971. More than 900 of them were teachers.

In addition to all this, Canada gives away some $90 million worth of food every year to needy countries. A recent example is afforded by drought in West Africa. Canadian planes and servicemen helped distribute nearly half a million tonnes of grain from all over the world to perhaps 30 million people. Fish, flour, and milk powder is given to foreign governments who sell it to their people and then use the revenue to finance their own development schemes.

Finally, Canada gives $50 million worth of commodity aid each year in the form of export credits on raw materials and fertilizers for use in developing countries.

In the 1960s the United Nations stated that all the developed countries of the world should try to supply perhaps 1% of their Gross National Products to the needy countries of the rest of the world. GNP is the total of all the wealth produced in a country in a year.

5-4. If Canada's GNP in 1970 was $83 billion, did Canada achieve the U.N. target figure with total aid of $557 million in that year?

Finally, let us see where most Canadian aid goes.

5-5. Use the 1971 figures in Figure 5-3 to draw proportional arrows[11] on a world map. Have the arrows pointing in the right directions. Where will you point the arrow to show loans made to international development agencies?

To finish — a note of gloom. Foreign aid is not nearly as effective as it might be. Receiving countries waste a lot of it. As much as 75% of it is eaten up in administrative overheads. Fast-growing populations in many countries eat up the gains of modern development. The technology gap between rich and poor nations widens all the time, and it costs more each year to try and bridge it. The best that can be said for foreign aid since the Second World War is that it has marked time; that is, it has prevented the poorer parts of the world from becoming any poorer. But how long will that last?

6 The Golden Horseshoe

REGIONALISM

Towards the end came ice—a layer of it nearly 1.5 km thick. This great mass of frozen water was intimately mixed with boulders, sand, clay, and other products of erosion by glaciers. If man had been around and if the ice had been clear enough for the human gaze to penetrate its 1 500 metres' thickness, an astonishing scene would have been revealed far below. A continually changing landscape would have assumed forms that melted away as fast as they were formed—like patterns in a kaleidoscope the land beneath the ice surface would have been sculpted by irresistible forces, pressure and movement, from above and from the north. For obscure reasons—but perhaps the universe was unfolding as it should—the climate became more genial, and the ice melted back faster than it could readvance. Glacial debris rained down on the landscape beneath only to be picked up by the rivers that became the colour of milk with all the silt that they carried. Boiling and eddying, these glacial meltwater streams carried billions of cubic metres of the landscape down to an immense hollow now filling up with a great lake which thousands of years hence would be called Lake Iroquois.

On a raw, barren land appeared spikes and sprouts of green. Pines and hardwood trees grew tall on the land which was slowly heaving itself upward after having borne an awesome weight for thousands of years. Lake Iroquois shrank in size as mammoths and prehistoric bison and deer, elk and bear of many now-extinct species roamed the land. Men appeared and hunted them for food or gathered nuts, roots, and berries. As they scoured the land for sustenance, one day the forest wall thinned abruptly to reveal to astonished eyes the wide, flat surface of Lake Ontario.

Over the years, high sand and clay bluffs had been attacked by storm waves on the lake. Currents had carried the debris west to form a long sand bar, or spit, across the mouth of a bay into which two rivers emptied from extensive marshes. Using a short, overland route from Georgian Bay, the early peoples of Ontario sought the protection of this bay for their birchbark canoes while they set camps on shore. They set their shelters as far from the marshes and bothersome mosquitoes as possible and met friends socially, traded, hunted, or fished. They called the place "Toronto" or "meeting-place." Lord Bathurst in the eighteenth century was to set up a British military post as far from the burdensome mosquitoes as possible: midway between the rivers Don and Humber. His choice of site is preserved in the name of a street in Toronto today. The British military presence was established at the foot of Bathurst Street.

European settlement was swift, thorough, and efficient. The ancient hardwood forest was cut down and burned. The pioneers came in by boat to various points along the shore of Lake Ontario. In those days Niagara Falls marked the head of navigation, and the western end of Lake Ontario was a terminus for a long time. Prosperity was quickly wrung from the land and attracted many people to the area. Today it is an area of great wealth. Many

N

0 _____ 25
scale km

Ontario

L. Simcoe

York

L. Scugog

Peel

Toronto

Halton

L. Ontario

Wentworth

United States

Niagara

Ontario	York	Peel	Halton
1 Brock	1 Georgina	1 Albion	1 Esquesing
2 Mara	2 Gwillimbury E.	2 Caledon	2 Nassagaweya
3 Pickering	3 King	3 Chingacousy	3 Burlington
4 Rama	4 York Reg. Mun.	4 Toronto Gore	4 Oakville, etc.
5 Reach		5 Mississauga	

Wentworth

Niagara

6 Scott	1 Ancaster	**Toronto**	1 Lincoln W.
7 Scugog	2 Beverly		2 Wainfleet
8 Thorah	3 Binbrook	1 Etobicoke	3 St. Catharines
9 Uxbridge	4 Flamborough E.	2 Scarborough	4 Niagara Reg. Mun.
10 Whitby E.	5 Flamborough W.	3 York	5 Lincoln
11 Whitby	6 Glanford	4 York E.	6 Grimsby
12 Oshawa	7 Saltfleet	5 York N.	
	8 Hamilton	6 Toronto	

Figure 6-1. The counties and 1971 census divisions of the Golden Horseshoe.

industries have come to the region, attracted by a number of factors, one of which is labour supply. As well, people have been attracted to the western end of Lake Ontario by the chance of finding a job. To several million people, the area is truly "the Golden Horseshoe."

6-1.   Lay a sheet of tracing paper over the map in Figure 6-1. Use the population density data in Figure 6-2 to establish a system of graded shading.[14] Use this graded shading to colour in the map on tracing paper.

Ontario		*York*	
Brock	12.5	Georgina	52.3
Mara	12.0	Gwillimbury E.	38.2
Pickering	111.5	t King	38.8
Rama	6.9	t York Reg. Mun.	117.1
Reach	14.5		
Scott	12.7	*Toronto*	
Scugog	16.2	t Etobicoke	2 281.0
Thorah	11.7	t Scarborough	1 822.0
Uxbridge	18.3	t York	6 354.5
o Whitby E.	38.6	t York E.	4 927.8
o Whitby	177.1	t York N.	2 850.4
O Oshawa	1 663.3	T Toronto	7 336.9
Wentworth		*Peel*	
h Ancaster	87.4	t Albion	20.4
Beverly	21.0	Caledon	17.2
h Binbrook	34.6	t Chingacousy	98.7
h Flamborough E.	52.5	t Toronto Gore	22.4
h Flamborough W.	70.9	t Mississauga	699.0
h Glanford	66.4		
h Saltfleet	197.2	*Niagara*	
H Hamilton	2 517.3	Lincoln W.	21.9
		Wainfleet	25.2
Halton		SC St. Catharines	1 161.9
t Esquesing	35.1	sc Niagara Reg. Mun.	297.8
Nassagaweya	18.2	Lincoln	87.2
h Burlington	399.1	h Grimsby	231.5
t Oakville etc.	336.2		

Figure 6-2.   The density of population in southern Ontario census subdivisions, 1971. All figures in people per sq. km.

Population growth has continued unchecked in the region for many years. Indeed, immigration to the Golden Horseshoe has continued to be encouraged as good for jobs, industry, people, and progress.

At the beginning of permanent settlement, towns and villages were small. Transportation was poor; the railways couldn't serve everywhere, it wasn't profitable. A fairly well-off person rode a horse, although the roads were dreadful in spring, while a poor person had to walk everywhere.

When you think about it, though, there was no need for large towns and cities. Most people were farmers and lived on their land. All they required was a market not too far away for their products, as well as for buying things that they could not make themselves. Then came a change. Industry grew up and made greater demands on manpower. Marginal farmers left the land and sold up to go and work in the city. Gradually the cities and towns extended their boundaries but not too much. People were unable to travel very far to their work. Although by the end of the nineteenth century streetcars served many rural areas, people still thought in terms of walking to work.

And then an urban explosion took place. Urban growth accelerated.

6-2. What technological revolution in transport took place about 70 years ago? Why did it accelerate the process of urban growth?

If you re-examine the map that you drew for assignment 6-1, you will notice that the densely peopled parts of the Golden Horseshoe are all along the lake shoreline and that they have a tendency to touch or run into one another. In Toronto, for example, Etobicoke houses might end on one side of a street and York houses begin just across the road. The dividing line between the two "towns" is the centre line of the road.

6-3. Examine Figure 6-2 again, this time paying attention to the prefix letters that occur in front of most of the census subdivisions.

H = Hamilton   T = Toronto   SC = St. Catharines   O = Oshawa

These upper case letters refer to actual cities. The same letters occurring in lower case refer to the fringe or suburbs around the cities where population densities are still quite high but not nearly so low as in the surrounding countryside.

Trace a map from Figure 6-1 and shade the census subdivisions as follows:

H = dark blue	h = light blue
T = dark red	t = light red
SC = dark green	sc = light green
O = dark yellow	o = light yellow

Name the four cities on your map.

The map that you have just drawn is one which shows "Census Metropolitan Areas" in the Golden Horseshoe. A CMA is really a convenience for people who have to organize the censuses of Canada. Instead of being organized by counties, the census planners try to take into account real things like cities rather than abstractions such as county lines or township lines.

6-4. Why is it a good idea for all the people in a CMA to band together when thinking of providing all the services that have to be provided, but which have to be paid for? For example, sewers, schools, garbage collection, police forces, etc.

Can you see anywhere on the map that you drew for assignment 6-3 where county lines are ignored in favour of closer ties with a city?

On reflection, the Golden Horseshoe is rather an odd place for several million people to live. It possesses no valuable raw materials such as coal, gas, oil, diamonds, gold, or other precious minerals. Power supplies have to be sought farther afield each year. There are virtually no timber resources left which would support even a fraction of one percent of the residents of the region.

Two advantages of the region are its fertile soils and mild climate. The Golden Horseshoe is at about the latitude of the Po valley in northern Italy and is able to grow such crops as grapes for wine, peaches and other fruits, and tobacco. Of course, with so many people around, there is getting to be less and less land available for growing crops in the Golden Horseshoe. In fact newspaper writers and commentators of all types bemoan the fact that every year more and more of the best agricultural land in the province—never mind the Golden Horseshoe—is taken over for roads and urban development. One particularly hot controversy rages over the Niagara escarpment. This is a steep slope facing east across the province of Ontario. It is composed of limestone, a hard, white rock laid down under tropical seas many millions of years ago. Too steep for much farming, it has been the target of conservation activity: many people object to housing developments there or the quarrying of rock for use in the building trade. Quarrying is highly visible and conflicts, say the conservationists, with the use of the escarpment for recreational purposes. They would like the Ontario provincial government to freeze any further encroachment for commercial purposes on this irreplaceable natural asset.

Nonetheless, people flock to the region in great numbers. Sixty thousand people a year have been coming to Toronto recently, and they must be housed. Land and home prices have soared in the last few years in the major cities of the Golden Horseshoe, and so many people have tried to buy homes beyond the city limits that the price of real estate has risen greatly even there. This makes it more profitable for developers to bid for land outside the city to build housing subdivisions, shopping plazas, etc. Some people would call this "urban sprawl," while others would welcome it as an attempt to provide for a clear need. A recent study shows that over half the people in Toronto live in rented accommodation because they cannot afford a home of their own. Yet many would purchase one if they could, even if it meant travelling much farther to work each day.

Year	Farm acreage (hectares)
1921	9 161 498
1931	9 247 327
1941	9 063 960
1951	9 263 180
1956	8 048 440
1961	7 521 663
1966	7 217 022
1971	6 462 776

Figure 6-3.   The change in the land area farmed in Ontario, 1921-1971.

6-5.   Calculate the percentage change in farmland for each year given in Figure 6-3, using 1921 as 100% each time. Plot your figures on a single-line, time-series graph.[8] What alarms you most about the graph? Is that necessarily bad? What do you think the situation will be like in 50 years' time?

As we have already mentioned, the natural resources of southern Ontario and the Golden Horseshoe are chiefly soil and climatic advantages. In addition, there are immense human resources (labour and skill) and great capital resources (factories and roads). It is the human and capital resources which today continue to attract people. These resources have come to the Golden Horseshoe to take advantage of its position.

The region penetrates deep into the heart of North America and occupies a central position. It is therefore well suited to manufacture products from imported raw materials and act as a distribution centre for them.

The Golden Horseshoe lies along the Great Lakes–St. Lawrence Seaway. Hamilton and Toronto both possess fine natural harbours which are in the process of being extended. Ocean freighters and lakers use both ports. Hamilton's steel industry uses Labrador iron ore, and coking coal from Pittsburgh which arrives via Cleveland on Lake Erie and the Welland canal. Toronto's cosmopolitan nature has resulted in finished products being imported from all over the world.

Railroads and highways from the west of Canada must sweep north of the Great Lakes but they naturally swing south to service the Golden Horseshoe. The land route to Montreal and the St. Lawrence lowlands is now traversed with a fine, modern highway. The route to New York via the southern shore of Lake Ontario and the valleys of the Hudson and the Mohawk are also traversed by fast expressways.

6-6.   Draw a sketch-map to show the position of the Golden Horseshoe and its function as a focus of routeways. Emphasize its central position in North America by putting on direction arrows pointing to New York, Montreal, Detroit, Chicago, Washington, and Indianapolis. Measure the straight-line distances represented by these arrows and write them beside the arrows in terms of kilometres.

7 Immigration

During the great Ice Age which began a million or so years ago, nearly all of Canada was covered over by huge glaciers. The glaciers scraped away soil from some areas and dumped it in others; they caused rivers to be diverted; they gouged out hollows which later filled with water to form lakes; they depressed some land below the level of the sea; and they carved deeper and wider valleys in mountain areas. During all this time there were no people living in Canada.

As the climate eventually changed and the glaciers began to melt away, and as the land began to be colonized by plants and animals, the first immigrants began to arrive. They were the Indians coming from the south and living in close connection with the plants and animals; the time was probably about 10 000 years ago.

The last places for the permanent ice to melt away were the far northlands, and these were accordingly the last places to be settled by immigrants coming after the Ice Age. The Eskimos came in across Alaska about 3 000 years ago.

Neither the Indians nor the Eskimos made any mark upon the land; they used it but they did not alter it. They lived at the mercy of their environment. And they lived this way for centuries, according to the "ways of their people."

Things began to change, however, when the Europeans first came. The Europeans introduced all sorts of new factors, like forts and firearms, religion and trade, and new ways and new technology. They introduced, above all, the possibility of shaping the environment to suit what the people wanted rather than what the environment determined. It is because of this capacity to produce material progress and change that we can call the immigrants beginning with the Europeans *resources.*

The development of the human resources in Canada has been a slow process. For one thing, the mother countries in Europe for years treated Canada as a colony to be exploited for its natural resources rather than as a country to be developed with its own human resources. And thus it was not really until Canada achieved nationhood in 1867 that a large degree of control over her own destiny became possible.

Throughout this entire period Canada has encouraged immigration. At times it has encouraged immigrants from certain places; at other times it has encouraged immigrants who have particular skills, wherever they come from. The reasons why Canada has encouraged immigration are fairly straightforward:

1 Canada wants more people to help populate the unsettled or sparsely populated areas. For example, when the Prairies were being opened up in the early 1900s the likely immigrants of eastern Europe were being tempted by offers of transportation to Canada for $1. Even now the Canadian government will lend money to people to pay their way to Canada.

2 Canada wants more people to help make its domestic market larger and thereby permit its manufacturing industries to gain some *economies of scale.*

Economies of scale means that it's often cheaper per unit to make a lot of things than it is to make only a few. For example, it would be relatively costly per unit to manufacture only a few cars, because you would still have to pay for all the tooling up, the factory, paint shop, and so on; whereas if you could make a lot of cars they would be cheaper per unit because the costs which you had to incur could be spread out over more cars. This is one reason, of course, why it pays Canadian manufacturers to export to other countries whenever they can; but it is also a reason why Canada encourages immigration — to enlarge its domestic market.

3   Canada wants to achieve a greater degree of economic independence for itself. A larger population would give Canada more independent force in dealing with other countries.

4   Canada wants to obtain new ideas, new customs, new techniques, new skills, and new enthusiasms. And these tend to come with new people, so immigration is again encouraged.

1900	41 681	1920	138 824	1940	11 324	1960	104 111
1901	55 747	1921	91 728	1941	9 329	1961	71 689
1902	89 102	1922	64 224	1942	7 576	1962	74 586
1903	138 660	1923	133 729	1943	8 504	1963	93 151
1904	131 252	1924	124 164	1944	12 801	1964	112 606
1905	141 465	1925	84 907	1945	22 722	1965	146 758
1906	211 653	1926	135 982	1946	71 719	1966	194 743
1907	272 409	1927	158 886	1947	64 127	1967	222 876
1908	143 326	1928	166 783	1948	125 414	1968	183 974
1909	173 694	1929	164 993	1949	95 217	1969	161 531
1910	286 839	1930	104 806	1950	73 912	1970	147 713
1911	331 288	1931	27 530	1951	194 391	1971	121 900
1912	375 756	1932	20 591	1952	164 498	1972	122 006
1913	400 870	1933	14 382	1953	168 868		
1914	150 484	1934	12 476	1954	154 227		
1915	36 665	1935	11 277	1955	109 946		
1916	55 914	1936	11 643	1956	164 857		
1917	72 910	1937	15 101	1957	282 164		
1918	41 845	1938	17 244	1958	124 851		
1919	107 698	1939	16 994	1959	106 928		

Figure 7-1.   Numbers of immigrant arrivals in Canada, 1900-72.

7-1.   Using the data in Figure 7-1 construct a time-series graph[8] to show the fluctuations in immigration to Canada. Can you suggest any reasons for the various ups and downs? Which were the chief decades of growth?

It has generally been one of Canada's constant policy requirements regarding new immigrants that they be able to cope on their own and not become a burden on the state. Canada has wanted resources, not liabilities; it has therefore forbidden anyone to enter who may have certain diseases or certain crippling abnormalities. It has equally forbidden entry to anyone with a criminal record in their own country (except for political refugees), and it has tended to deport immigrants who break certain laws in Canada. Don't forget: Canada wants resources not liabilities.

For this reason, Canada has required that immigrants generally be of at least the same broad level of achievement as resident Canadians in such fields as education, job training, professional skills, and personal qualities. In the period 1962-1967 Canada accordingly began to change the basis of immigrant entry from its old quota system (so many from here, so many from there) to its new points system. Immigration officers around the world were instructed to assess potential immigrants and award points on the basis of:

1 Education and training, one point for each full-time year up to a maximum of 20.

2 Personal qualities, such as motivation, adaptability, and initiative, up to a maximum of 15.

3 Occupational demand within Canada, up to 15.

4 Occupational classification, on a scale of 10 for a professional person down to 1 for an applicant with no skills.

5 Age, on the basis of 10 for a person up to the age of 35, less 1 point for each year over 35 years of age.

6 Arranged employment, up to 10 points for a job with a signed contract.

7 Knowledge of French and English, up to 10 points depending upon fluency.

8 Employment opportunities in area of destination, up to 5 points for a strong demand.

9 Relatives, up to 5 points for a relative already in Canada who is prepared to help the immigrant settle in to a new country.

7-2. Construct a percentage bar graph[3] of the information on the points system.

The new points policy meant that Canada no longer specifically sought immigrants from particular places. Instead immigrants began to be accepted in increasing quantities from Asia and the West Indies rather than just Europe and the U.S.A.

	Europe	Asia	U.S.A.	West Indies	Other
1960	79	4	11	1	5
1961	73	4	15	2	6
1962	72	3	15	2	8
1963	76	4	13	2	5
1964	73	5	11	2	9
1965	74	7	11	1	7
1966	75	7	9	2	7
1967	72	9	9	4	6
1968	66	12	11	5	6
1969	55	14	14	9	8
1970	51	14	17	9	9
1971	43	18	20	10	9
1972	42	19	19	8	12

Figure 7-2. Immigrants to Canada, percent, by major areas of former residence.

7-3. Construct two divided circle graphs,[5] one for 1960 and one for 1972, to illustrate the data in Figure 7-2. In addition, calculate index numbers[6] for 1972 for each of the four major sources of immigrants, using 1960 as the base (e.g., for Europe the 1960 figure is 79%; if we call this base 100, then the 1972 figure of 42% becomes an index of 53.2). Which source of immigration has grown the fastest?

London	Cologne	Tel Aviv
Manchester	Hamburg	Beirut
Birmingham	Stuttgart	New Delhi
Glasgow	Vienna	Istanbul
Belfast	Budapest	Tokyo
Dublin	Belgrade	Hong Kong
Paris	Stockholm	Manila
Bordeaux	Lisbon	Sydney
Marseille	Madrid	Port of Spain
Brussels	Rome	Kingston, Jamaica
Berne	Milan	New York
The Hague	Athens	Chicago
Copenhagen	Cairo	San Francisco

Figure 7-3. Canadian immigration and information offices around the world.

7-4. Plot the centres mentioned in Figure 7-3 on to a world map. Which parts of the world are significantly without Canadian immigration offices?

One of the big problems with a non-racial points system based on education and skill is that, while it may be good for Canada to thus obtain highly qualified manpower relatively cheaply (because some other country has paid for the education and training), it is not necessarily good for the countries that lose the immigrants. In particular, some of the highly qualified people from the poorer countries in the world see Canada as a land of opportunity for themselves but fail to realise at the same time that the countries they are leaving are going to be short-staffed in several important areas. For example, poor countries can ill afford to lose doctors and teachers, but they lose them anyway. Canada is thus developing a bit of a reputation around the world for skimming off the cream!

all data are in percent

	1	2	3	4	5	6	7	8	Canadian average
professional	35.9	32.8	7.7	8.3	34.2	1.2	30.9	45.4	26.6
clerical & service	36.6	12.6	13.0	44.8	21.7	13.0	29.8	18.3	26.6
construction	2.0	1.8	17.4	7.4	0.8	24.4	6.5	2.8	6.5
manufacturing	12.6	18.2	36.0	27.4	14.8	30.1	17.6	8.7	19.8
general labour	1.1	1.7	9.0	1.5	1.7	1.8	0.6	0.8	2.1
others	11.8	32.9	16.9	10.6	26.8	29.5	14.6	24.0	18.4

1: China, including Hong Kong and Taiwan

2: India

3: Italy

4: Jamaica

5: Pakistan

6: Portugal

7: U.K.

8: U.S.A.

Figure 7-4. Occupational classification of immigrants, selected countries, 1971.

7-5.   Draw a series of eight horizontal percentage bar graphs,[3] directly underneath one another, from the information in Figure 7-4. Write down the thoughts that occur to you as you examine the figures.

". . . most of the American immigrants chose Canada because of the quality of life . . ."

". . . they thought life in Canada would be pleasanter . . ."

". . . I can't imagine going back. This is a better place to live . . ."

". . . the demand for professionally qualified and skilled people from overseas is unending . . ."

". . . there are all kinds of openings, ranging from aeronautical engineers and geophysicists to physical therapists and librarians . . ."

". . . of course, it is the children that Canada is interested in, for even if the parents don't become Canadian in outlook the children certainly will . . ."

It was in 1973 that the points system came under official review. The immigration minister at Ottawa decided that Canada's policy perhaps needed to be changed a little, but he wasn't sure how. So he asked the Canadian people to start a great public debate about whether more immigration was needed and if so, then what sort should be encouraged. The debate is still going on. Indeed it will always go on, because Canada can't build a wall around itself to keep others out. What do you think?

8 Land Use

MAN THE CHOOSER

Before the coming of the Europeans to Canada there were perhaps a quarter of a million people in the country already. They are the people we know today as the Indians and Eskimos. With very few exceptions these people were much more closely bound by nature than the people who inhabit Canada today. Their food-gathering activities were much less efficient than those employed by the Canadians of the twentieth century. They lived by hunting, fishing, and gathering nuts, herbs, berries, fruits, and roots from the forest. Of the tremendous mineral wealth of Canada they had little or no inkling because at their level of technology they had little or no use for it. They were stone age in culture. Very few of these first people were permanently settled. Mainly they were bound to travel from one well-established area to another as the seasons changed and as the supply of animal and plant food and material ebbed and flowed in tune with the seasons.

Nearly 500 years after the coming of John Cabot, Canada has been greatly transformed. One of the greatest differences is the way in which Canadians support themselves. There were more than 22 million of them in 1973, and they enjoy a very high standard of living. This can be directly attributed to the type of steel and energy culture they practise. In turn, this has led to the land being used differently from the way the Indians and Eskimos used it.

A major change in the use of the land is that a larger proportion of it is cultivated. Many happy gnawers at corn-on-the-cob are unaware that this plant was cultivated by the Huron Indians in what is now Ontario. It was grown under a form of shifting agriculture since the corn fields were quickly exhausted by monoculture and an almost complete lack of fertilizer. The actual land area that was used to grow corn at any one time was very small. It could hardly be otherwise. The Indians had no machinery and only the crudest forms of digging sticks. Also, there were never very many Indians.

The land area of Canada is 997 614 000 hectares. This is nearly 6 percent of the total world land area. The land area of Canada used for growing crops is 4.4 percent and a further 2.1 percent is under pasture.

8-1.   How many hectares did each Indian have before the coming of the European settlers? How many hectares does each Canadian have today? How many hectares of agricultural land does each Canadian have today? Show your answers by means of proportional rectangles drawn on graph paper.

8-2. For the purposes of international comparison, consider the following information:

Country	Population	Total land area	Agricultural land
China	800 000 000	956 100 000 hect.	30.0 percent
U.S.	200 000 000	936 145 000 ,,	47.4 ,,
Japan	100 000 000	36 988 000 ,,	17.7 ,,
U.K.	55 000 000	24 203 000 ,,	80.4 ,,

Construct proportional shapes on graph paper to show the amount of agricultural land an inhabitant of each of the above countries has, including Canada. Do you think Canada is well off in terms of land to provide food?

Stand by for a shock! As you no doubt realize, not everyone in any country is a farmer. Far from it. Yet the people who are farmers or farm workers must provide food for all the people in the country. Sometimes they cannot, of course, and some food supplies must be imported. Nevertheless, they try their best with the land and facilities they have available.

Country	Agricultural land area ('000 hectares)	Agricultural population (thousands)	Total population (thousands)
U.S.	443 733	11 700	200 000
China	287 300	500 000	800 000
India	177 890	350 000	600 000
Netherlands	2 210	1 050	10 000
U.K.	19 620	2 100	55 000
Japan	6 551	23 000	100 000
Italy	20 227	12 000	55 000
Brazil	137 034	40 000	85 000
Pakistan	28 358	84 000	115 000
Egypt	2 835	16 000	30 000
Australia	490 614	1 100	12 000
Canada	64 845	1 700	22 000

Figure 8-1.   Selected agriculture and population data. The figures have been rounded for population.

8-3. Calculate the agricultural land area per farm worker and the percentage of total population that is agricultural from the data in Figure 8-1. Construct a scatter graph[7] to show your answers. When you have drawn this scatter graph you will see that there is a very wide spread of points. Australia especially will be hard to plot. But you will see that some countries have very little land per farm person and that more than half their people farm. Put a red line around that group. Then put a blue line around those countries which have a lot of land area per farm worker but very few people employed in agriculture. The last group, to be circled in yellow, is of countries which do not have very many of their people in agriculture, certainly well under half of them. Yet the countries are so small and the total populations are so large that the land area per farm worker just has to be very limited. Here are three labels for the three groups: extensive agriculture, intensive agriculture, subsistence agriculture. Write the correct label beside each group on your graph.

Extensive agriculture produces a lot of crops. It can't fail to do this because so much land is planted. However, because the farm workers are spread so thinly, the output of crops from any one hectare is usually not very high. There would have to be a lot more people working in agriculture in order to raise the production per unit area.

On an intensive farm, the opposite is true. There is no shortage of labour, only a shortage of farmland. So the people working on the farms have to use every little piece of land and as much fertilizer, pesticide, and machinery as they can afford.

On a subsistence farm the people are short of everything and are usually too poor to do anything about it.

Well, which sounds like Canadian farming to you?

8-4.   Canada, India, and the Netherlands — three different types of farming.

India has 60 000 tractors and uses about 1 700 000 tonnes of fertilizer per year.

The Netherlands has about 150 000 tractors and uses about 615 000 tonnes of fertilizer per year.

Canada has 600 000 tractors and uses about 755 000 tonnes of fertilizer per year. Calculate how much fertilizer that is per hectare and how many hectares there are per tractor for each of the above countries. Do the results surprise you?

How would per capita GNP figures of $3 130 for Canada, $2 160 for the Netherlands, and $80 for India help to explain the results?

8-5.   India produces 20 093 000 tonnes of wheat from 16 626 000 hectares.
Canada produces 9 023 000 tonnes of wheat from 5 052 000 hectares.
The Netherlands produces 634 000 tonnes of wheat from 142 000 hectares.

For each of the above countries, draw proportional shapes on graph paper to show areas cultivated, wheat production, and yields. Be sure to use the same scale for each country. Again, do the results surprise you?

Well, not everyone is a farmer in Canada. What about all the other people in Canada? Where do they live? In towns and cities, of course! Now, you can live in the country and not farm. You might commute to the city to work, or you might be retired, or you might even be able to work out of your home. As a matter of fact, 76 percent of Canada's people live in urban areas and the remaining 24 percent live in rural areas. The inhabited area of Canada is 420 000 sq. km. The total land area is about 10 million sq. km. About 2.5 percent of the inhabited area is made up of cities and towns, that is, built-up areas.

8-6.   On graph paper, construct a rectangle to represent Canada's total land area. Mark off how much of it is inhabited. Inside that area, mark off how much is built-up area.

What is the population density in the uninhabited areas of Canada? In the towns and cities? In the remainder of the inhabited area?

Finally, the forests. Out of a world total forested area of 4 091 million hectares, Canada's forests occupy 443 094 000 hectares. They constitute an important renewable resource which contributes greatly to the Canadian economy.

8-7.   What percentage of the world's forests is possessed by Canada?

8-8.   Construct a divided circle[5] to show, in Canada,

  i) the arable land area
  ii) the pasture land area
 iii) the built-up land area
 iv) the forested land area
  v) other remaining land area.

What sort of land do you think the other remaining land area is? Describe it.

Doubtless as the means by which we create wealth change, so will the pattern of Canadian land use. As a matter of fact it is changing all the time. People buy and sell land for different purposes all the time. It was different in the past from what it is today and of course it will be differently used in the future. Perhaps the biggest change will come to the northern areas of Canada. All kinds of plans are afoot, not only to develop the mineral wealth and natural resources but even to settle people there.

Whatever happens in the future, though, just remember that land use reflects changing hopes, cultures, and economies.

9 The Mid-Canada Corridor

SUPPORT OF LIFE

Unlike most countries in the world, Canada still has a frontier. It lies in the Canadian Northland, waiting for . . . what? Before we attempt to tackle that question, let us try to imagine what the north is like. Probably we all picture the north differently and yet our pictures surely contain some points of similarity. Ice, minerals, snow, mosquitoes, tundra, wildlife, forests, solitude. What do think of when you read the words "Canada's Northland?"

The idea of a frontier raises the image of relatively few people tackling nature or at least coming to terms with it. That is certainly true in Canada's case, for the great mass of Canadians live along the U.S. border. Nearly one-third of Canada's people live within an hour's car ride of Toronto. The distribution of Canada's population is very uneven, but of course there are good reasons for this. What can you think of?

Despite the attractions of Canada South as a place of work and residence, technologically it is possible for people to live the same kind of lifestyle they now enjoy but one thousand miles north. Just think what the north has to offer: clean air and water, plenty of open space and cheap land for housing, and unlimited recreational opportunities. So why haven't more people gone to live farther north?

The reasons are partly economic and psychological. The greatest number of jobs in Canada today are in the so-called tertiary sector of the economy — service industry. This has little to do with churches or car maintenance but mostly with the servicing of people; for instance insurance, banking, serving in a restaurant, selling subway tokens. Selling services to people can form one's livelihood only if there are large numbers of people around. And people are some of the things that the north has in short supply. Before you decide that it would be a good idea to encourage, push, drive, or entice more people to go north, just bear in mind that Russia has had the same kind of problem with Siberia for centuries, and that new cities in Siberia were achieved only with the kind of political and social system that has evolved in Russia since 1917, and even then at the price of suffering and hardship of the early developers and colonists of the region. Before the Russian revolution, Siberia was used as a dumping ground for a variety of offenders against the state and society.

It is unthinkable that Canada would force people into developing the north or that the north would be used as a kind of detention centre. Instead, companies and the government pay bonuses and northern allowances to individuals willing to forgo the attractions of Canada South. Even then, many people just go north for a few years to work and save with an eventual view to returning home. The money attracted them but the psychological burden of changing one's outlook and lifestyle to adjust to small-town life (most northern towns are very small) proved too much.

> 9-1. To help you perceive better where most of Canada's people live, plot the extent of Canada's ecumene, or inhabited, developed area on a map obtained from your teacher. Obviously you need your atlas to help you! The ecumene is seen on a map as a variable-mesh net composed of railroads, highways, canals, and other transport routes which are knotted together with towns and cities. The edge of this net is ragged and discontinuous.

In 1971 the Mid-Canada Development Conference met to focus attention on, and highlight the potential of, the Mid-Canada Corridor. An MCDC report was issued which stressed the advantages of choosing the boreal forest belt of Canada as the site of the MCC. Canada possesses 22 percent of the world's softwood resources and 17 percent of the world's freshwater surface area. In addition there are great mineral reserves, both known and only guessed at. The MCC would stretch across these riches for perhaps 5 000 km. It would cover an area of 2 600 000 square km, an area larger than Western Europe.

> 9-2. On the map that you drew for assignment 9-1, plot the extent of the boreal forest belt of Canada.

As you are now aware, the boreal forest belt is already partly incorporated in the ecumene of Canada. Very few people live there as yet but the the ones that do work mainly in primary industry such as lumbering and mining. There is a little tertiary industry in the form of stores and government representation, as well as tourism. Secondary or manufacturing industry is scarcest of all since it depends on large, local labour forces.

A significant exception is the paper industry. It makes sense to process the timber into pulp and paper as close to the forests as possible. Why is that? There are already more than 20 mills in operation in the boreal forest belt and it is estimated that there could be at least another 40, each employing 1 000 people.

> 9-3. If each mill employs 1 000 people and each person supports a family of 2.3 on average, how many people are dependent on paper-making now? Potentially how many paper workers and dependants could the boreal forest support?

In addition to lumbering, of course, mineral extraction is well advanced, and prospecting for fresh riches to be consumed by metal-hungry western technology has never been so intensive. Names like Copper Cliff, Uranium City, and Yellowknife speak for themselves. Don't they?

The reasons for a lack of secondary industry are not complicated. There are few if any local markets. Raw materials would have to be shipped in and the finished products shipped out. In addition, labour costs would likely be higher than in Canada South, because living costs at the moment are quite high in the north. This is unfortunate but is caused by firms being unable to achieve *economies of scale*. It costs as much if not more to build a super-

The boreal forest: northern Alberta.

market in Kapuskasing, Ont., as it does in a southern city, and nearly as many staff have to be hired. Yet the population of Kap. is only a few thousand, and they all work in the Kimberley-Clark paper mill there or depend on incomes from it. Therefore the turnover of a store in Kap. will be quite small compared with a comparably sized store in Toronto. So the profit per item has to be higher for the store to become a paying concern. Also, the store's stock has to be freighted in for quite a few hundred miles. This all adds to the cost.

If more people lived there, living costs would fall. But more people won't live there *until* living costs fall. It is a vicious circle. How can it be broken?

So much for economics. A lot of people are put off a northern life by their picture of the climate there. What do you think the climate of the boreal forest belt would be like?

	J	F	M	A	M	J	J	A	S	O	N	D
Goose Bay, Newfoundland												
Temperature °C	-18	-16	-9	0	4	10	16	14	9	3	-5	-13
Total Precipitation cm (of which snow)	3.8	6.0	6.1	4.5	5.3	6.4	8.3	6.9	5.6	6.1	6.4	6.3
	(3.6)	(5.7)	(6.0)	(3.7)	(2.0)				(0.2)	(2.3)	(4.9)	(6.2)
Knob Lake, Quebec												
	-24	-22	-14	-6	1	9	13	11	6	-1	-9	-18
	4.0	4.0	4.8	3.5	3.2	7.9	8.9	8.8	7.8	7.5	6.4	3.1
	(4.0)	(4.0)	(4.7)	(3.0)	(2.0)	(0.8)			(2.3)	(3.6)	(5.4)	(2.8)
Kapuskasing, Ontario												
	-18	-17	-10	-1	8	14	17	16	11	4	-5	-13
	5.1	3.5	4.2	4.2	5.8	7.1	8.4	8.1	8.2	5.4	6.0	5.3
	(4.9)	(3.3)	(3.6)	(2.1)	(0.6)				(0.1)	(0.9)	(4.0)	(4.9)
Thunder Bay, Ontario												
	-13	-12	-6	2	8	14	17	17	12	6	-3	-10
	5.8	3.6	5.0	5.5	6.7	10.5	7.3	9.3	8.5	6.6	6.4	5.2
	(5.4)	(3.5)	(4.1)	(2.8)	(0.2)					(0.4)	(2.8)	(4.5)
The Pas, Manitoba												
	-21	-18	-11	1	9	14	18	16	11	3	-8	-17
	2.0	2.0	2.1	2.4	3.5	5.8	6.1	5.8	5.2	2.8	2.9	2.5
	(1.9)	(2.0)	(2.0)	(1.4)	(0.2)					(0.9)	(2.7)	(2.5)
Edmonton, Alberta												
	-13	-12	-5	4	11	14	17	16	11	5	-4	-11
	2.3	2.0	2.2	2.8	4.6	7.5	7.9	5.8	2.9	2.1	2.3	2.4
	(2.2)	(2.0)	(2.0)	(1.5)	(0.4)				(0.3)	(1.8)	(2.0)	(2.3)
Fort Simpson, N.W.T.												
	-26	-23	-16	-4	7	14	17	14	8	-1	-14	-24
	1.9	1.6	1.1	1.3	2.7	3.5	4.9	4.1	3.4	2.0	2.3	2.0
	(1.9)	(1.6)	(1.1)	(1.0)	(0.4)				(0.2)	(1.2)	(2.3)	(2.0)

Note: snow in rainfall equivalent.

Figure 9-1. Selected climatic data.

9-4. Use the climatic data in Figure 9-1 to construct small climatic graphs[13] located correctly on a map of Canada obtained from your teacher. Beside each named climate graph, write down the number of months at or above freezing. Mark on the limits of the boreal forest. Well? How would you like the climate of the Mid-Canada Corridor? How does it compare with what you are used to?

That part of the MCC which lies on the Canadian Shield (an undulating plateau of very old, hard rock) is of very great importance for all of Canada. It is in this region that Canada's greatest hydro-electric power stations send energy humming along high tension wires to feed the great urban and industrial areas of the south. Here also are Canada's potential HEP sites. Vital though they are, these great power stations provide little direct employment in the immediate area except during construcion. The James Bay project in Quebec, for example, is slated to provide several thousand construction jobs in the four or five years that it will take to complete the project. To maintain and oversee the completed project will require the labour of only a few hundred people permanently.

Ontario	s.r.	Quebec	s.r.	Manitoba	s.r.
Ottawa	0.6	Upper Ottawa	0.5	Winnipeg	0.6
Madawaska	0.3	Lower Ottawa	0.6	Saskatchewan	0.7
Abitibi	0.5	Upper St. Lawrence	1.0	Nelson	1.0
Mississagi	0.3	St. Maurice	1.0	Laurie	0.1
Mattagami	0.4	Bersimis	0.9		
Montreal	0.1	Manicouagan	0.5		
Nipigon	0.5				
English	0.3				
Kaministikwia	0.2				
Winnipeg	0.2				
Aguasabon	0.2				

Note: s.r. numbers are derived from both installed capacities and averages of power outputs on an annual basis. Data are given only for the three most prominent provinces. The locations are rivers within the named provinces and represent the sums of all HEP stations to be found along them.

Figure 9-2. Hydro power in the boreal forest belt of Canada.

9-5. On a blank outline map of Canada, locate the boreal forest belt. Then, using the s.r. numbers in Figure 9-2, construct located, proportional circles[4] to show the sizes of HEP stations at the locations shown. If the most accessible sites for HEP have nearly all been developed, shade in on your map the areas where you think the remaining (potential) sites are.

Give two reasons why the winter months present a challenge to the generation of HEP.

If one theme has emerged from this study of the reality and the potential of the Mid-Canada Corridor, it is probably on the lack of people. We shall now examine a little more closely this question of population.

	Boreal forest population	Total population
Yukon	13 000	18 000
Newfoundland and Labrador	20 000	522 000
North West Territories	25 000	35 000
British Columbia	100 000	2 185 000
Alberta	600 000	1 628 000
Saskatchewan	60 000	926 000
Manitoba	40 000	988 000
Ontario	700 000	7 703 000
Quebec	700 000	6 028 000

Note: boreal forest populations are estimates only.

Figure 9-3.   Mid-Canada populations, 1971.

9-6.   Obtain a map outline of Canada from your teacher. Be sure that it has the provincial boundaries marked on. Calculate the percentages of the provinces' and territories' populations which live outside the present limits of the boreal forest belt. Show your answers by means of located percentage bar graphs.[3] If you can, suggest why the percentages differ so much.

And that's it! The MCC is not at all an easy area to sum up in one phrase or sentence. It is far too vast and varied for that. But since the concept or idea behind this section is "Man the Chooser," perhaps the aspect that the MCC presents to most Canadians is a negative one — at the moment. However, Prime Minister Trudeau may have proved to be a prophet when he said, in the early 1970s, "Go north, young people, and grow up with the country." Well, what is *your* choice?

10 The Moving of Freight

SPATIAL INTERACTION

Did you know that about 40 000 tonnes of paper bags are moved by Canadian railways each year? And that about 85% of them originate in Quebec? And, while you can probably guess that most of the paper bags (about 65%) go to Ontario, did you know that the province with the second largest receipts of paper bags is New Brunswick (about 10%)? Can you guess why New Brunswick ranks second?

If we look at something a little different from paper bags, say live cattle instead, then we find that Canadian railways ship about 125 000 tonnes each year. The live cattle come chiefly from Alberta (about 40%), Saskatchewan (25%), and Manitoba (20%), and go mostly to Ontario (about 85%). So that gives us Ontario relying on Quebec for paper bags and the Prairie Provinces for live cattle! Conversely, of course, both Quebec and the Prairie Provinces rely on Ontario to act as the market for their produce.

We can trace out linkages of this nature for every classification of railway freight that Statistics Canada uses, and that's over 300 categories. However, we don't want to go into all that detail right now; so let's just select out a few classes which will tell us how the railways help to make the different provinces and regions of Canada dependent upon one another. We've already noted how Quebec relies on Ontario to buy its paper bags and, equally, how the potato farmers of New Brunswick rely on Quebec paper bag manufacturers to supply them with suitable bags. And we've also already seen how western farmers rely on eastern markets and how eastern consumers rely on western food producers — at least for cattle products. So let's now take a look at a few other important products.

	a fish	(s.r.)	b wheat	(s.r.)	c potatoes
Nfld.	+250	15.8	—	—	−30 000
P.E.I.	+250	15.8	−2 000	44.7	+44 000
N.S.	+7 500	86.6	−35 000	187	−1 400
N.B.	+15 000	122	−150 000	387	+10 000
Que.	−7 500	86.6	−80 000	282	−18 000
Ont.	−16 000	126	−18 500 000	4301	−15 000
Man.	−2 500	50	+2 000 000	1414	−5 500
Sask.	−750	27.4	+18 500 000	4301	−400
Alta.	−2 000	44.7	+3 800 000	1949	−2 500
B.C.	+25 000	158	−5 200 000	2280	−12 000

	d lumber	e agricultural machinery	(s.r.)	f cars	g electrical appliances
Nfld.	−68 000	—	—	−900	−2 100
P.E.I.	−3 000	−1 000	31.6	—	−500
N.S.	+6 500	−1 500	38.7	−11 700	−2 300
N.B.	+33 000	−2 700	52.0	−37 700	−3 600
Que.	+135 000	−8 000	89.4	−215 000	+7 500
Ont.	−715 000	+80 500	282.8	+500 000	+30 700
Man.	−67 000	−8 400	91.6	−47 700	−10 000
Sask.	+22 000	−22 000	148.3	−48 300	−3 400
Alta.	+300 000	−19 000	137.8	−70 000	−17 700
B.C.	+5 220 000	−6 900	83.1	+21 200	−10 500

all figures in tonnes
+ = shipped out
− = received in

Figure 10-1.   Approximate net balance of product movement by rail freight, 1972.

10-1.   Using the data in Figure 10-1 prepare a series of seven positive-negative vertical bar graphs,[20] one for each commodity shown. Write seven short paragraphs describing briefly what *each* bar graph shows you; and then write an eighth paragraph to say what all the seven bar graphs *together* tell you about the economy of Canada.

10-2.   Using the s.r. numbers for column *a* in Figure 10-1, construct proportional circles[4] on a map of Canada. Shade the circles as follows: those provinces with a net outward movement (+) red, those with a net inward movement (−) pale yellow.

10-3.   Using the s.r. numbers for column *b* in Figure 10-1, construct proportional circles[4] on a map of Canada. Shade the circles as indicated in assignment 10-2. Can you explain the very high net inward movements to Ontario and British Columbia?

10-4. Using the s.r. numbers for column *e* in Figure 10-1, construct proportional circles[4] on a map of Canada. Shade the circles as indicated in assignment 10-2. When you look back at your answers to assignments 10-2, 10-3, and 10-4 what can you say about the different provinces of Canada?

The amount of freight carried by the railways is not only extremely large and varied but it is also increasing rapidly year by year. In 1960 for instance, the total was about 180 million tonnes; in 1965 it had risen to about 240 million tonnes; and by 1970 it had reached 270 million tonnes. In order to cope with the increasing volume of freight, and to offer better service and cheaper freight rates as well, the railways have been developing a number of modern *aides.* Computers to control yard marshalling and to assist in car location (so that any consignment of goods can be instantly located any-where in Canada) are now fairly commonplace. So are unit trains. Unit trains were first developed in America in 1962, but the idea was readily adopted by both CN and CP. The basic idea is more than just shipping a trainload of uniform product. Canada has been doing that for years with its wheat trains to Thunder Bay. What the unit train means in addition is that the train is never pulled apart; it remains a unit at all times. When it is filled with whatever it is scheduled to carry (wheat, coal, iron pellets, sulphur, or whatever), it just rolls along to its destination, by-passing all yards. When it gets to its destination (a port, a mill, or whatever) it is unloaded, sometimes without even stopping, and then it returns empty to wherever it gets filled up again. And then it repeats the process . . . again . . . and again . . . and again. It's almost like a rolling, pulsing, pipeline, with one-way freight move-ment only. The coal trains from the Crow's Nest Pass down to Roberts Bank are a good example; so are the iron ore trains from Schefferville and Labrador City down to Sept Iles. The Labrador City line also has another unusual feature: it has a ten-kilometer feeder line with a completely automated unit train. No crew.

Pipelines don't have a crew either; nor do they have crashes or go on strike. They are therefore considered to be ideal for moving fluids in bulk, like oil, gas, water, and petroleum distillation products. They are also con-sidered to be a good prospect for moving solids like coal, iron, and sulphur, which can be powdered, mixed with oil or water, and pumped along as a *slurry.* Inco already does this at Sudbury, where it pumps nickel-copper con-centrate 15 kilometers along a pipeline. The very high cost of installing pipelines is to some extent offset by the lack of "crew," and by the avoidance of any need to return empty cars or trucks. Operating costs are therefore fairly low.

There are five main pipeline systems in Canada at the moment. Three are for the transmission of gas: the *Alberta Gas Trunk Line* gathers gas from a variety of sources in Alberta and then delivers it to the *Trans-Canada Pipe Line,* which takes it east all the way to Toronto and Montreal; and in addition some is taken westwards into British Columbia via the *Westcoast Transmis-sion pipeline.* And two are for the transmission of oil: the *Interprovincial Pipe-line* gathers oil from the western Prairies and carries it to Sarnia and Port Credit; and the *Trans-Mountain Pipeline* takes oil from Edmonton to Van-couver. Another smaller oil pipeline supplies Montreal from Portland in Maine.

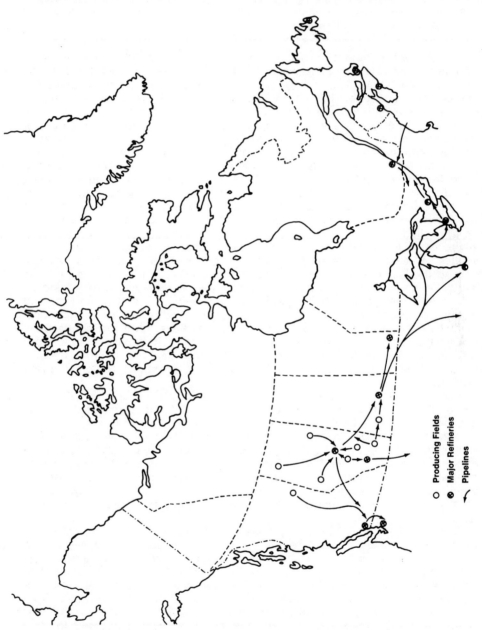

Producing Fields

Major Refineries

Pipelines

Figure 10-2. Crude oil pipelines and refineries in Canada.

all figures in millions of litres

	crude oil production	crude oil used	transported out of province: to Canadian markets	to U.S. markets
domestic:				
B.C.	4 200	7 500	—	12 000
Alta.	66 200	7 200	{ 15 300 to B.C. { 39 700 to Sask.	
Sask.	14 200	3 200	50 700 to Man.	—
Man.	900	2 600	27 000 to Ont.	22 000
Ont.	100	22 000	—	5 000
imported:				
Que.	—	25 500	100 to Ont.	—
N.B.	—	4 000	—	—
N.S.	—	4 000	—	—
P.E.I.	—	1 500	—	—
Nfld.	—	4 000	—	—

Figure 10-3.   Distribution of domestic and imported crude oil, 1971.

10-5.   Using the map in Figure 10-2 as a guide (TRACE YOUR OWN! !), and the data in Figure 10-3 as basic information, construct a flow-line map[18] to illustrate the movements of crude oil through Canadian pipelines. Make sure that the width of the flow-lines (or flow-bands, as they may sometimes be called) is proportional to the amount of crude oil.

Another important way of moving commodities in bulk is by canal or river transport. The chief canal by far is the St. Lawrence Seaway, which was opened in 1959 partly with a view to providing Canada with a fourth "ocean access" frontier (what are the other three?). The high hopes of the early canal builders have never been fully realised, but there is still a large amount of cargo (approximately 75 million tonnes in 1971). Even so this is less than the traffic which is confined just to the upper Great Lakes (especially Superior and Michigan).

	tonnes
agricultural products:	23 000 000
— of which —	
wheat	10 000 000
barley	5 000 000
corn	3 500 000
soybeans	3 500 000
mineral products:	35 000 000
— of which —	
iron ore and pellets	20 000 000
coal	11 000 000
salt	1 500 000
processed products:	16 000 000
— of which —	
steel	5 000 000
fuel oil	4 500 000
scrap iron	1 000 000
other freight:	1 000 000
Total:	75 000 000

Figure 10-4.   St. Lawrence Seaway traffic, 1970.

10-6.   Using the information in Figure 10-4, construct a divided circle graph[5] to illustrate the importance of bulk cargo to the St. Lawrence Seaway.

	tonnes upbound	tonnes downbound
domestic:		
Canada to Canada	8 000 000	15 000 000
Canada to U.S.A.	14 900 000	20 000
U.S.A. to Canada	50 000	20 000 000
U.S.A. to U.S.A.	550 000	780 000
foreign:		
Canada imports	1 000 000	—
Canada exports	—	1 500 000
U.S.A. imports	5 500 000	—
U.S.A. exports	—	7 700 000
totals:	30 000 000	45 000 000

Figure 10-5.   St. Lawrence Seaway traffic orientation, 1970.

10-7.   This is a hard one: can you design a flow-line (flow-band?) map[18] of the Seaway region (Lake Erie down to the St. Lawrence below Montreal) to show all the data in Figure 10-5? If you try to do a good job with this, we'll call this the last assignment in this study! Good luck.

But before we let you go, you should take a look at Canada's northern river — the Mackenzie. Mackenzie himself called it the River of Disappointment, but people now have a different view. Then, however, Mackenzie was disappointed because his river didn't flow into the Pacific; nowadays people are quite delighted that it flows into the Arctic. Because if it didn't there would be a real problem in getting supplies to the western Arctic (the eastern Arctic isn't a problem in this respect, because supplies can be readily shipped from Montreal or St. John's, but the same ships cannot easily get through to the western Arctic because of ice).

The navigation season on the Mackenzie is quite short: a few weeks in summer only. Even in June and July there may be ice on Great Slave Lake (get your atlas out and have a look at its location), though the Mackenzie itself is usually free of ice then because of its fast-flowing waters. In that short season all the supplies for the Northland are pushed down river by steel-hulled diesel-powered tugs. The carriers are giant steel barges with capacities up to 750 tonnes each, linked together in barge trains. The trains run from Hay River on Great Slave Lake to Tuktoyaktuk on the shores of the Arctic: the journey takes about two weeks.

The only other ways to get supplies to the north are either piecemeal by air freight or intermittently by winter-truck line. Air freight is important in getting emergency or urgent supplies to the north and is absolutely and literally vital in getting any sort of supplies at all to some of the more isolated communities. Did you know, for example, that it takes about 20 tonnes of material to support a non-Eskimo for a year in the north, and that 75% of that is fuel? Air-freighted fuel is a pretty important cargo to some people. As for trucks, the only highway north is the Mackenzie Highway, which runs all the way north to Yellowknife (look at your atlas again). North of Yellowknife the best way to get truck traffic through is to drive it over the frozen ground in winter. Winter roads are quite common, but in summer they turn to unusable mud. Naturally, goods cost more north of Yellowknife.

11 The Moving of People

SPATIAL INTERACTION

Some of you may never have been on a railway.

At one time ("once upon a time . . .") you would have been. The first railway in Canada was built in 1836 to connect the water transport systems on two rivers (the St. Lawrence and the Richelieu). After that there was a period of slow railway growth; people considered them as best-suited for linking water routes and acting as alternative winter transportation. It was not until the 1850s and 1860s that people really began to get interested in this new-fangled invention, but it was not until Confederation that the nation as a whole got involved. One of the promises made to British Columbia, for instance, to persuade it to join Canada rather than the U.S.A. was the construction of a transcontinental railway. This was finished in 1885, and you can read about it in Pierre Berton's books, *The National Dream* and *The Last Spike.* By the time the Pacific coast had been brought into rail contact with central Canada the whole of Canada "from sea to sea" was linked by steel. The network was built up mostly in the Ontario-Quebec district, but it gradually spread across the Prairies, where the railway companies were granted land in return for carrying in settlers. Eventually the railway mesh came to mark out the limits of the settled areas of Canada, with only a few loose edges, as it were, running off into the northern wilderness (such as to Churchill on Hudson Bay, or to Moosonee on James Bay, or to Pine Point on Great Slave Lake).

Within the railway network as it now exists, all 100 000 kilometres of it, there are many different types of track. Some is multiple track, designed for heavy commuter use, in and around major urban areas such as Montreal. Some is double track, busily and frequently used, lying in major transportation corridors between major metropolitan areas, such as that between Toronto and Montreal. It is on this particular stretch of busy inter-city track that Canadian National runs its most frequent and fastest train services, notably the *Rapido* and, when it works, the *Turbo.* It is on a similar (but much more densely populated) route in southern Japan that Japan National Railways runs its famous bullet trains (on special track though: the C.N. trains run on regular track, which means they cannot go so fast). Some of Canada's railway track is single, long-distance line, as on most parts of the transcontinental routes. Schedules are so open that there is no demand for trains going in opposite directions to pass frequently, so that loop-sections will do for this. However, since it takes five days or so to cross Canada by rail, there is not too much demand from passengers for more frequent services. Yet another type of track is that which winds out into scenically attractive country or country which will in some way interest tourists. The Algoma Central line north of Sault Ste. Marie, though also carrying iron ore and lumber, makes a big promotion out of carrying tourists to Agawa Canyon (and back). Tourists come from all over North America to travel on this line. Another popular tourist line is the Ontario Polar Bear Express run by the Ontario Northland Railway to Moosonee, though this too serves a commercial function as well, supplying the isolated communities of northern Ontario. The White Pass and Yukon line is another popular tourist rail route, this time across the coastal mountains of northern British Columbia.

A rather special, and still expanding, form of passenger rail transportation is city subways. These are separate from the other rail systems (at the moment), but they are no less important for carrying people about. If it were not for the Toronto subway system, for example, most of the downtown workers (about 70% or so) would have real difficulty in getting to and from work every day. Indeed it is likely that if it were not for subway availability, the large downtown offices would have to be more scattered across the metropolitan area.

There are 24 separate railway companies in Canada, dominated by Canadian National (50% of all traffic) and Canadian Pacific (40%), and even though they are still vastly important in the movement of people they are not so important as they once were. And, additionally, the movement of people is not so important to the railway companies as it once was.

Rolling stock data (1970):

	Number of locomotives	3 417
	Number of passenger cars	2 801
	Number of freight cars	204 928

Traffic data:	a (freight in millions of tonnes)	b (passengers in millions)	c (Canada's population in millions)
1920	129.4	51.3	8.6
1925	111.7	41.5	9.3
1930	117.0	34.7	10.2
1935	78.3	20.0	10.8
1940	112.2	22.0	11.4
1945	170.5	53.4	12.1
1950	167.0	31.1	13.7
1955	191.5	27.2	15.7
1960	181.7	19.5	18.2
1965	241.5	23.1	20.0
1970	265.3	23.8	21.3

Figure 11.1   Selected railway data, 1920-1970.

11-1.   Draw a simple ordered bar graph[1] to show the information relating to rolling stock in Figure 11-1.

11-2. Using the information in columns *a* and *b* of Figure 11-1, construct a time-series graph[8] to show the changes in freight carried, 1920-70, and in passengers carried, 1920-70. You will clearly have to use different scales; so put the freight scale on the left vertical axis and the passenger scale on the right vertical axis. Use two contrasted but *pale* colours for the two lines. Then: divide column *a* by column *b*, multiply by 100 to obtain a percentage-based ratio, and plot the results on your graph by means of a third BRIGHT line and a BRIGHT scale set up on the inner (right-hand) side of the left vertical axis. Label all three lines directly: do not (repeat, not) use a legend. Can you think of the purpose of this third line? What are your conclusions?

11-3. The third line you drew on your graph in 11-2 would (or should) have told you just how passengers have declined in importance in comparison to freight as far as the railways are concerned. But the pale line you drew in to show passengers carried could possibly have left you a little confused. There is a decrease from 1920 down to 1940, but then passenger traffic picks up again to a peak in 1945, only to decline again to a low in 1960, when it again picks up. Doesn't seem to make sense, does it? Would you care to try to explain these ups and downs? Perhaps a class discussion on the topic would help.

11-4. If you want to get a really effective idea of just how *relatively* unimportant rail transportation has become for passengers, then calculate column *b* in Figure 11-1 as a percentage of column *c,* and plot your answers on a time-series graph.[8] Does the fact that the percentages are all over 100 tell you anything? What does it mean when the percentages drop closer to 100, as they have recently started to do?

Over the years since 1920 the average distance of a passenger journey by rail has increased from about 100 kilometres to about 200 kilometres. This does not mean that most people are now travelling farther than they used to; what it does mean is that the railways have lost most of their local short-haul passenger traffic (they still have some, of course, like the Montreal suburban commuter traffic and the Toronto GO commuter traffic). Nevertheless, short journeys are now made by means other than rail for the most part. Cars and buses have captured most of the short-haul market, as well as quite a lot of the medium-haul and even long-haul markets.

Data for privately owned passenger cars are not easy to obtain. We can fairly easily get information about the number of them, but that's about all. We don't know how far they all travel or where they all go, because travel is free across Canada (there are no check-points or customs posts) and no one collects any statistics. In consequence we are a little restricted in coming to any conclusions about car traffic; perhaps that's one very important reason why cars are so popular. They go where you want when you want (pretty well, anyway), and no one keeps a check on the journeys. Personal freedom in this instance acts a little against you: you have no solid facts!

	population, 1971	passenger cars registered, 1970
Nfld.	522 105	89 568
P.E.I.	111 640	30 376
N.S.	788 960	210 974
N.B.	634 555	159 307
Que.	6 027 765	1 602 129
Ont.	7 703 105	2 576 041
Man.	988 245	306 559
Sask.	926 240	284 251
Alta.	1 627 875	530 420
B.C.	2 184 620	811 590
Yukon	18 390	5 700
N.W.T.	34 805	4 200

Figure 11-2.   Population and car ownership.

11-5.   We can still get a rough idea of the relative importance of cars to people across Canada if we examine the data in Figure 11-2. To get it a little more precise, calculate the number of people per car in each province. Obviously the fewer people per car, the greater the degree of individual freedom to travel by car. Can you suggest any reasons for the relatively high figures for Newfoundland and the Northwest Territories?

Buses are another matter. People keep check on them, whether they are travelling on a line-route between set points (e.g., an urban bus route or an inter-city bus route) or on a chartered journey to wherever the customers want to go. Most cities are linked to each other by bus lines, such as the Greyhound, Voyageur-Colonial, Gray Coaches, Travelways, and Norton lines. And most cities also have student round-up and delivery services by way of school buses into the surrounding countryside. A breakdown of figures on a city-by-city basis is not possible, but some information is given in capsule form in Figure 11-3.

Passengers:
   regular routes —
      inter-city and rural   42 667 621
      urban and suburban   4 685 491
      inner urban transit   805 273 096
   special and charter service —   11 823 555

Bus kilometres:
   regular routes —
      inter-city and rural   181 245 320
      urban and suburban   4 077 518
      inner urban transit   316 305 200
   special and charter service —   4 901 957

Figure 11-3.   Passenger bus data, *Canada Yearbook, 1972.*

11-6. Draw two percentage bar graphs:[3] one to show the percentage composition of the passenger traffic, and the other to show the percentage composition of the kilometres covered. What conclusions do you draw about the differences shown?

Water transportation for people is nowhere near so important as it once was. In the early days of Canada's development (in, say, the 1600s, 1700s and early 1800s), water transportation was very important. Much of the interior of Canada was opened up and explored by water-travelling voyageurs, even as far west as the Rockies. In the east, proximity to the St. Lawrence and the Great Lakes was a paramount consideration; indeed, in early Quebec, the St. Lawrence was more or less like the main street, with people living on both sides and crossing it freely to visit each other. Since then, of course, things have changed: at first the railways took a lot of passenger traffic away from the rivers and lakes; then so did cars and buses at a later date. Nowadays, the only people who travel by water do so because they have to (excluding holiday travel, that is). These are the people who live on islands and require ferry connections to the mainland. The people of Newfoundland rely a lot on ferries (they don't depend entirely on them, of course: there are planes too), and so do the people of Vancouver Island. In between, there are smaller-scale services like the Toronto Island ferries, and the ferries across the St. Lawrence at Quebec-Levis. The largest ferry service in Canada (probably the largest in the world as well) is the British Columbia ferry service, which is vital as a link all the way along the B.C. coast and into the Gulf Islands. The ferries are often called the B.C. Navy!

Water transportation for fun is probably much more widespread, but there are no statistics. Nevertheless, just visit any of the lakes or waterways during the summer months, and you'll see (you've already seen, right?). One of the chief pleasure waterways is undoubtedly the Trent Canal system in Ontario, which is now maintained by the provincial government purely for tourists and at no direct cost to them.

all figures in $ millions.

	passenger revenue	freight revenue	total revenue*
1961	143.3	19.5	165.4
1962	158.8	21.9	183.5
1963	167.7	24.1	199.4
1964	177.1	27.7	213.9
1965	209.9	31.8	250.1
1966	243.9	36.9	289.9
1967	295.6	40.2	345.6
1968	328.1	50.9	387.6
1969	332.7	57.3	404.7
1970	387.5	56.1	478.3

*total revenue column contains a larger figure than the sum of the other two columns. This is because there are other revenues from excess baggage and mail.

Figure 11-4. Operating revenues for Air Canada, 1961-70.

One of the British Columbia ferries.

11-7. The operating revenues for Air Canada for the period 1961-70 are shown in Figure 11-4. They illustrate the rapid growth which is occurring in air transportation, and they also indicate the relative values of passenger and freight traffic. Construct a compound-line graph,[9] shading the passenger sector different from the freight sector. Which sector is increasing at the fastest rate?

Air transportation is perhaps one of the most suitable forms of long-distance people-moving in Canada. For a country with such vast distances and such a scattered population the airplane is ideal. The first noteworthy developments of air transport were in the 1920s, when pioneer bush pilots began to open up parts of the Northland. A number of local airlines serving more densely populated areas in southern Canada gradually developed during the 1920s and 1930s, but nothing was done to link the nation "from sea to sea" until an immigrant from the U.S.A. (C.D.Howe) founded Trans-Canada Airlines, which became Air Canada in the mid-1960s. TCA was started in 1937, and so coast-to-coast services with a single airline became possible. It was still necessary in those days, though, to change aircraft periodically, because they could not travel very far (or very high). The introduction of jet aircraft after World War II opened up longer route possibilities, and Air Canada, along with CP Air (which had been started during the war), began to develop overseas routes.

Within Canada, the two major "flag carriers" also act as local carriers, but they are supplemented in that role by a second level of regional carriers. These regional carriers are officially designated by the federal government, which keeps tight control over all air operations inside Canada. The five regional carriers are Eastern Provincial Airways, covering the Atlantic Provinces and operating out of Gander in Newfoundland; Nordair, covering much of northern Quebec, Ontario, and the Northwest Territories and operating out of a base in Dorval near Montreal; Quebecair, covering Quebec and Labrador and operating out of Montreal; Transair, covering Ontario, the Prairies, and the Northwest Territories and operating out of Winnipeg; and Pacific Western Airlines, covering most of northern and western Canada and operating out of Vancouver.

11-8. The scheduled (non-charter) flights of Transair are as follows:

a   Winnipeg-Regina-Saskatoon-Prince Albert-and return
b   Winnipeg-The Pas-Flin Flon-Lynn Lake-Thompson-return
c   Winnipeg-Gillam-Churchill-return
d   Winnipeg-Thompson-Churchill-return
e   Winnipeg-Norway House-return
f   Winnipeg-Brandon-return
g   Winnipeg-Dauphin-Yorkton-return
h   Winnipeg-Thunder Bay-Toronto-return
i   Winnipeg-Kenora-Dryden-Thunder Bay-Sault Ste. Marie-Toronto-return
j   Winnipeg-Red Lake-return
k   Churchill-Eskimo Point-Rankin Inlet-Baker Lake-return
l   Churchill-Coral Harbour-Repulse Bay-Hall Beach-return

Plot all these places on to a map of Canada and connect them up according to the route schedules for Transair. Use bright colours. Now you know at least a little bit about how one of the second-level regional carriers links Canada together.

Below the second level carriers are the third level carriers, though they hate to be called that. There are about 20-25 of them, and they act as local feeders to either the regional or the flag carriers. In Ontario, the provincial government sponsors a third level carrier called norOntair, which is operated for the government by White River Air Services. In Quebec, Air Gaspe is another local example; while in the west Time Air has developed a set of services linking all the cities of Alberta to each other.

And then there are nearly 500 *more* airlines in Canada. But these are mostly very small and lacking scheduled services. They operate on a charter basis ("You want to rent or hire a plane? Step this way . . ."). Many of them serve local communities in remote areas, acting as carry-alls, like the Reindeer Air Service at Inuvik, owned by Fred Carmichael, an Indian, and having an Eskimo, Tommy Gordon, as its chief pilot.

12 Newfoundland

THE SUPPORT OF LIFE

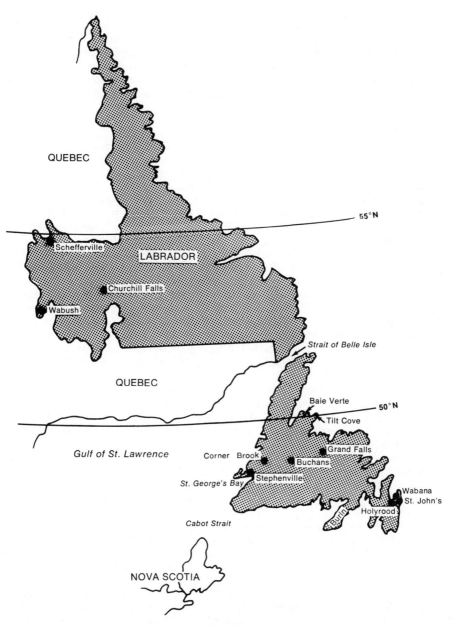

Figure 12-1. Places in Newfoundland.

If you looked hard enough you could probably find a Newfoundland restaurant that would give you a meal of cod tongues and seal stew. And if you didn't want to look too hard then you could probably find cod or turbot or sole or haddock easily enough — along with fiddleheads and blueberries, of course. But not wrapped in newspaper: after all, Newfoundland doesn't belong to Britain any longer. It's been part of Canada since 1949.

Ever since Cabot's discovery of the island in 1497, Newfoundland has had a close connection with the sea and its produce. Early use of the land by Portuguese, French, English, and other fishermen was mainly for rest, repair, and provisions. Indeed, for about 300 years after Cabot's discovery, people were forbidden by old-country "fishing admirals" from settling on the island. They intended that use of the island should be temporary (summer only) and not directed towards any sort of colonization. Needless to say, such a restriction was almost impossible to police adequately: people in fact did settle on the island. The settlement which was most widely accepted was St. John's, which existed as a repair and provision base as early as the 1500s, but gradually other settlements also came into being. The smaller settlements were not so widely accepted, and the people in them accordingly scattered themselves widely around the shores of Newfoundland in small communities sheltered not only from the sea but also from any policing vessels. These "outports" came to be located on remote islands or inside sheltered coves and bays, and as time passed and the settled population grew, more and more outports were developed to fill in any usable gaps in the shoreline fringe of settlements. By the early 1950s there were possibly 1500 outports of this nature, each with only a few families (at most, say, a hundred families, but more usually ten or twenty), all of whom relied directly on the produce of the sea for a living. The *inshore* cod fishery was the source of livelihood, exploited by a series of two-man dories with long baited lines. Every season the cod would be either eaten locally in one of a hundred different ways or salted and preserved for sale to the itinerant merchants who came round from St. John's. The St. John's merchants would then sell the salted cod to buyers in Africa, South America, and the West Indies. To supplement the cod diet, there would be a few locally grown vegetables, mostly potatoes, and milk from goats. Life was hard.

It was even harder if anything went wrong, because help was often far away, and both communications and transportation were very difficult. The chief form of access was by coastal vessel, which was not only slow even at the best of times but almost literally funereal if fog or storm or ice closed down the shipping lanes.

And education was not easy to obtain either. A Royal Commission on education estimated that children in the one-room schools of Newfoundland had one chance in 700 to complete secondary school. Illiteracy was not uncommon; therefore alternative means of livelihood were often difficult — if not impossible — to obtain.

In addition, a crisis began to develop in the 1950s. One reason for the crisis was the rapid growth of large *high-seas* fleets from other countries (chiefly the U.S.S.R., but also the U.K., Germany, and Denmark). These fleets did not fish the inshore areas; they fished the Grand Banks, but they took so many fish that the inshore stocks also became depleted. And the outporters accordingly began to go hungry. Catches of 1000 kilograms dwindled to catches of 400 kilograms and less. Another reason for the crisis was that Newfoundland had only recently joined Canada, and it wanted quickly to catch up to Canada's standards of health, education, and so on. In order to do this, the thousands of scattered outporters had to be collected together into a smaller number of larger and more profitable centres.

Accordingly, in 1954 the government began a program of re-settlement, bringing the outporters — often against their will — into 77 designated growth centres. The chief period of re-settlement was 1965-71, but the social and economic disadvantages that became evident gradually brought about an easing-off in the application of the program. The chief disadvantages were the unemployment that the re-settled people endured and the loss of a life-style that many people preferred.

Unemployment is probably the wost problem. The causes are varied, not least being the illiteracy of many outporters, but the lack of alternative employment opportunities is also a contributory factor.

12-1. In 1951 the population of Newfoundland was 361 416, of whom about 40 000 were outport fishermen. By 1972 the population had grown to about 532 000, of whom only 8 000 or so were outport fishermen. Show this information by means of two divided proportional circles[5] (s.r. of 361 416 is 601; s.r. of 532 000 is 729).

Even if there aren't many alternative opportunities available, there are at least *some.* So let's have a look at them. We've already hinted that some farming is carried out, but when we examine soil and climate data for Newfoundland we find that the picture is gloomy for expansion. Soils are generally poor: the hard rocks have not weathered into thick soils anywhere, and the thin soils which do exist are usually leached (leached?) and not very fertile. As for the climate, you only have to know that maximum daily temperatures in summer barely reach 15-16°C to realize that any farming that is carried on must be very close to the margins of cultivation. Snow falls on average about 85-90 days each year in the centre of Newfoundland and about 65-70 days in the south. Compared with these figures, Montreal has only 62 snowy days, Charlottetown 48, Halifax 38, Ottawa 51, Toronto 45, Winnipeg 57, Calgary 54, Vancouver 12, and Yellowknife 53. The only agricultural product that Newfoundland is self-sufficient in is eggs. Everything else has to some extent to be imported. There is really no future in farming in Newfoundland.

Forestry was an early alternative activity. As early as 1909 a pulp and paper operation had been opened at Grand Falls, and since that time capacity has increased from 30 000 tonnes to 300 000 tonnes. However, the permanent workforce is only about 1 750, so large-scale opportunities do not exist there either. A second pulp and paper operation was started at Corner Brook in the early 1920s, with an annual capacity of about 200 000 tonnes. Subsequent expansion has brought the mills to a capacity of about 450 000 tonnes and a payroll of about $10 million a year. A third mill is now in operation at Stephenville, opened in 1973. However, for all these mills there is one over-riding consideration: they must compete on world markets to sell their produce. This means that they have to use the most efficient machinery they can; this in turn means that not so many workers are needed. Where the workers *are* needed is in the forests, but not too many seem to want to work there. Despite the high unemployment figures, forestry companies have thousands of vacancies for jobs in the forest. The workers seem to prefer staying with their families. As a result the lumbering operations are forced to employ as much machinery as possible, and the new mill at Stephenville even has to import some of its lumber needs from Labrador (though new stands are being developed in south-west Newfoundland). Forestry, therefore, could offer a

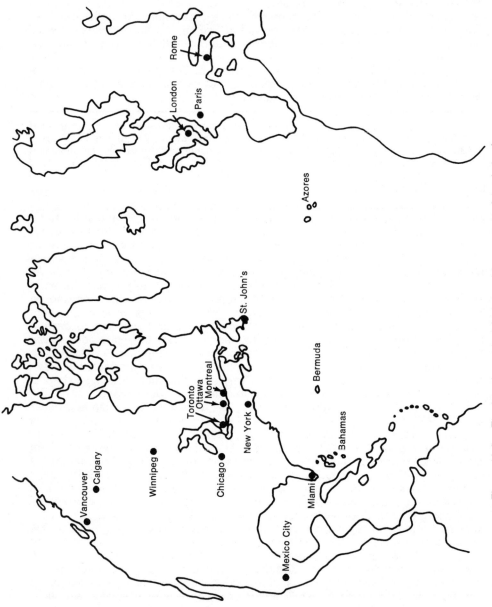

Figure 12-2. The location of Newfoundland in the North Atlantic basin.

viable alternative source of employment, but the people who want work seem not to want that particular kind of work.

Another early alternative activity was mining. The Asarco copper-lead-zinc mine at Buchans in the centre of Newfoundland was the first major development (1928) of the modern period; and it added to the older and richer Wabana iron mines on Bell Island near St. John's, which dated from 1898. Miscellaneous smaller mines produced other minerals, such as fluorspar in the Burin Peninsula, gypsum near St. George's Bay, copper and gold at Tilt Cove, and asbestos at Baie Verte. The most recent large-scale developments, however, have been off the island, in Labrador, where the gigantic iron mines at Wabush, Carol Lake, and Schefferville now form the main source of supply for the great North American steel industry.

Accompanying the developments in Labrador has been the mammoth hydro project at Churchill Falls, which was designed to produce nearly four times as much electricity as the Niagara Falls scheme. Because the island of Newfoundland is pretty well self-contained in electricity generation, the government contracted to sell the electricity to Hydro Quebec.

Power production seems to be a major theme for present development. In addition to the Churchill Falls Project, there are other large schemes which have now been built; the largest and most significant is the giant oil refinery at Come-by-Chance, but there are smaller ones at the Bay d'Espoir (hydro) and Holyrood (thermal electricity). The significance of the Come-by-Chance refinery lies in the choice of location: large deep-water accommodation for supertankers at a point suitable for distribution throughout the western Atlantic (see Figure 12-2). A smaller pioneer of this type of development was the Ultramar "Golden Eagle" refinery at Holyrood. You can look for more developments of this type, where the key thing is ability to serve a part-continental market.

And the products don't always have to be bulky, like oil. They can be small too, like electronics goods. For example, resistors are now made at Stephenville, for distribution to the eastern half of North America. Further expansion can be seen when you consider that Newfoundland is the closest part of North

America to Europe; if products are made in sufficient quantities to gain the economies of long production-runs, then access to the European market becomes just as possible as access to the North American market. The sorts of products best suited for development in Newfoundland are either those which require space and deep-water ports (oil, paper, minerals) or those which require easy access to as wide a market as possible (specialized electronics goods, gourmet fish items, crab and lobster, fashion goods). And, of course, there are the packaging industries.

But we're now visualizing a Newfoundland vastly different from the one with hundreds of outports and a largely illiterate population. We're seeing one with a highly technical labour force and world-wide marketing links (but then, didn't Japan have to start somewhere at one time?).

12-2. The following figures are dollar values of Newfoundland's Gross Provincial Product and fish landings. Calculate fish landings as a percentage of GPP, and write down your results *and* conclusions. Don't forget those conclusions . . . they are very important!

	GPP in $	fish landings in $
1968	975 000 000	27 800 000
1969	1 075 000 000	28 200 000
1970	1 189 000 000	32 735 000
1971	1 310 000 000	32 550 000
1972	1 540 000 000	30 425 000

---

	a	b	c
Nfld.	532 000	1 540 000 000	7 983 321 000
P.E.I.	113 000	317 000 000	249 574 000
N.S.	794 000	2 532 000 000	3 640 363 000
N.B.	642 000	2 093 000 000	5 167 208 000
Que.	6 059 000	24 951 000 000	62 909 225 000
Ont.	7 825 000	42 200 000 000	61 508 401 000
Man.	992 000	4 400 000 000	8 727 961 000
Sask.	916 600	2 663 000 000	5 442 238 000
Alta.	1 655 000	8 100 000 000	9 986 629 000
B.C.	2 247 000	11 870 000 000	25 226 853 000

a Population (1972 estimate)
b Gross Provincial Product in $, estimated (1972)
c Electricity output in kilowatt-hours, (1972 estimate)

Figure 12-3. Selected data, Canadian provinces.

12-3. Canadians, even including Newfoundlanders, have a tendency to think of Newfoundland as a poor province. Using the data in columns *a* and *b* in Figure 12-3, calculate the Gross Provincial Product per capita for each province, and then draw an ordered horizontal bar graph[1] of the results, shading Newfoundland in blue and all the rest in pale red. Is Newfoundland a "have-not" province? How do you think it stacks up against other parts of the world? Look at the information in Figure 12-4 and then look at your answer about Newfoundland being a "have-not" province again!

Australia	2500	Italy	1500
Bangladesh	100	Japan	1500
Belgium	2200	Kuwait	3750
Brazil	350	Libya	1100
Chile	570	Mexico	570
Congo Republic	80	Netherlands	2000
France	2550	Saudi Arabia	380
Germany	2200	Sweden	3300
Greece	800	Switzerland	2750
India	90	United Kingdom	1860

Figure 12-4. Selected world GNP figures, United Nations *Statistical Yearbook,* 1971.

12-4. Using the data in columns *a* and *c* of Figure 12-3, calculate each province's electricity output per capita. What do you notice about the position of Newfoundland? What do you think this means for the future?

---

13 The Northland

CHANGE

"In one corner of the room the children were glued to the new colour TV. It was Saturday night, and an exciting hockey game was being received via the world's first domestic communications satellite. In another corner of the room the parents were talking and reading quietly. They preferred picture magazines, and their talk occasionally reverted to their native tongue. Upstairs the old couple had already gone to bed: they were tired, and, besides, they did not understand English. The old man listened to his wife sleeping: and he dreamed himself of the old days ... days when he had gone out with four or five others on a hunting expedition, perhaps to return only after several days when sufficient food had been caught. At least now, he thought, there is enough food, and life is not so hard and precarious. But he wondered at the same time whether he felt as satisfied as he used to. He couldn't answer this; and eventually he drifted off to sleep."

Change has been occurring for a long time in the Northland. It started perhaps about 3000 years ago when the great glaciers of the Ice Age were dwindling away in the north and the Alaskan Eskimos were beginning to colonise the Canadian Arctic. The imprint of man had begun. For *nearly* the next 3000 years the Eskimos lived a hard, subsistence life. They had to pursue their food completely; there were no grasses or herbs, fruit trees or bushes, nuts or vegetables. Just running animals, swimming fish, and flying birds. At different times, the Eskimos relied more on animals than on fish, and at other times they relied more on fish than on animals. Their habitations were therefore sometimes inland, sometimes coastal, and sometimes both. The basic pattern throughout, however, was of a series of centralized meeting places where all the members of a kinship group could assemble every so often, after spending varying periods of time out in the dispersed hunting camps or actually on the hunt. Numbers were at all times small, at most perhaps about 20 000, though no one really knows.

Then came the Europeans. They came at a time when the Eskimos were in one of their maritime phases and so contact was readily established. The first Europeans were explorers from England looking for the North West Passage to the Orient. Their memory exists today in the names of many of the features of the Arctic: Frobisher Bay (1576), Davis Strait (1587), and Hudson Bay (1610), for example. After 1670 the Hudson's Bay Company was very important in *fur*thering contact with the Eskimos and the northern Indians, and significant changes began to occur in the life and philosophy of the Eskimos. The introduction of new weapons to the trappers (especially rifles and metal traps) greatly increased the "take" of animals, which were now hunted for fur and profit instead of solely for subsistence; the introduction of trade meant a breakdown of the traditional ideas of isolation and group independence, and the increasing dependence of the northern peoples on a higher level outside civilization gradually changed the location of their meeting places from wherever they happened to have been functionally centralized to wherever the Hudson's Bay Company trading post happened to be located. The entire basis of life was beginning to shift.

But even though major changes had begun, they were still happening very slowly. One of the main reasons for the slowness of change was the failure of the HBC to find the North West Passage, the Arctic thereby remaining a backwater rather than becoming a routeway (as the searchers had hoped). Attempts to find the Passage continued, however, and it was one of the spectacular failures to find it that really began to open up the Arctic. In 1845 the experienced Arctic explorer Franklin was commissioned to go yet again and try to find the Passage. He led a lavishly equipped expedition. And he failed again. In fact, he failed even to return: he had to abandon his ships in the ice, and he died in 1847. In England there was considerable concern over his failure to return; search-and-rescue expeditions were sent out over the next ten years until the remains of his expedition were found. In that time, the Arctic was explored quite thoroughly, and good navigation charts were made and published.

As a result of this exploration the northern waters were opened up more fully to the commercial whaling fleets which already operated around their edges (Davis Strait and the Beaufort Sea, for example). The pace of change began to quicken in devastating fashion. One of the chief results of the whaling fleets coming into the Arctic was wholesale disease among the Eskimos. The fleets often wintered in the Arctic, and the prolonged and massive contact between the sailors and the Eskimos caused many deaths to the Eskimo. The Eskimo population was approximately halved. The whales suffered also: they were hunted *almost* to extinction, and the declining numbers around the turn of the century eventually made Arctic whaling uneconomic, so the whaling fleets withdrew. And the Eskimos, who had relied on the whales as part of their maritime culture before the whaling fleets moved in, were left without an effective maritime life support system.

A renewed interest in the land-based resources of the Arctic was fostered by the HBC, which built up the white fox trade. The Arctic fox now replaced the whale in the trade-oriented economy of the Eskimos, and the pattern of dependence upon outside markets continued. Along with the white fox, the muskrat was also important. It was trapped by Eskimos and northern Indians in all the swamp and delta lands which abound in the north. Living was again reliable, but perhaps not so exciting as when whales were hunted.

One of the chief countries engaged in the whale trade had been Norway, and one of Norway's main explorers — Sverdrup — was busy at the turn of the century claiming uninhabited Arctic islands for Norway. The Canadian government was not very happy about this. In consequence the RCMP was sent up to establish stations along the coast, and special government-financed *Canadian* expeditions were sent out, like those of the *Neptune* and the *Arctic*. Federal interest was beginning. Another major change was under way.

In the 1920s and 1930s there was a flurry of local developments. Mining discoveries were made in the Northland (for example, oil at Norman Wells, radium at Great Bear Lake, gold in the Yellowknife district), and the outside world began to enter the Northland in larger and more permanent numbers. Transport and communications began to be developed. For example, the first bushplanes entered the Arctic in 1921, and the first back-up ground radio stations were established (by the federal government) in 1923. The railway from the Prairies stretched out to Churchill in 1929. And the federal government

A new style Eskimo.

decided that it would be a good idea if the Eskimos could be persuaded to start settled herding so that they could develop a reliable local supply of food without having to depend on unreliable trapping, so the federal government bought a herd of reindeer in Alaska and had it driven 2500 kilometres to the Mackenzie delta. The drive took five years! The government had high hopes, but the Eskimos didn't take to reindeer herding at all. It proved to offer an unexciting alternative to trapping for trade, and the Reindeer Station in the Mackenzie delta only just survives today as an example of a good idea which failed.

Eventually, World War II occurred and government interest in the Northland was spurred to further action. With American help the government built new airfields (to act as staging posts to and from Europe), expanded the radio links, and experimented with roads. After World War II there was a bit of a slump. Eskimos and Indians who had worked in air bases lost their jobs, and the white fox fashion trade declined. An attempt was made to develop the sealskin trade to replace the fox trade, and for a while this succeeded. By the early 1960s, for example, seal shipments outvalued fox shipments. But the outcries of conservationists, naturalists, and others resulted in a decline of the seal trade. The polar bear was then given a turn at being pushed commercially, but there are not many polar bears, and conservationists want to protect them too. The current commercial animal is the musk-ox. In 1973 the Northwest Territories and the government of Alberta fought each other (with words) over which area ought to have the full commercial rights to the products of musk-oxen. The people of the Northwest Territories claimed, with some justification, that they were running out of animals which they could use and that they didn't have as many alternatives for development as the people of Alberta.

Meanwhile, other changes were occurring as well. A cold war had developed between the U.S.A. and the U.S.S.R., and ballistic missiles had been invented. The Americans began to take what we considered an over-zealous interest in our Northland, since that is the closest part of the continent to Russia and the place over which any U.S.A.-bound aircraft or missiles would pass. In order to offset both threats (Russian attack from over the Pole and American take-over from the south) the Canadian government worked to set up a chain of radar bases across the Northland. Subsequently a chain of weather stations was also set up. The installation and maintenance of these bases provided not only work for Eskimos but also a great advance in their exposure to high technology.

The federal government expanded its activities by deliberately trying to get Eskimos to settle in areas which the federal government regarded as superior to those where the Eskimos already were. For example, Eskimo volunteers were persuaded to move north into unsettled land on the northern islands. Resolute Bay Eskimo Community was thus founded in 1953 next to Resolute Bay air base, while another group was settled at Grise Fiord in 1956. The advantages of these moves were, to the Eskimos, richer game sources and, to the federal government, a Canadian presence in the High Arctic. There are now a great many small settlements strung out around the Arctic shores, all with federal government sponsorship. Some are a success, like Grise Fiord, but some are a failure, with welfare being the main means of livelihood. The general result of federal government re-settlement plans has been to empty the countryside of Eskimos and Indians. The countryside, always thinly populated, is now emptier than ever of people, but the small villages are bursting with people.

The life basis of these newly permanent villagers is quite different from what it used to be. From independent subsistence hunting and functionally centralized meeting places, the Eskimos have moved through a period of dependence on outside traders (whalers, furriers, and so on) and settlements located around trading posts into, now, a period of dependence on federal assistance and government-determined settlements.

But things are continuing to change. At the Cape Dorset community in southwest Baffin Island, for example, the Houstons, who arrived in 1951, fostered the development of what was to become one of the most unusual settlements in the world: a community where the citizens earn their living

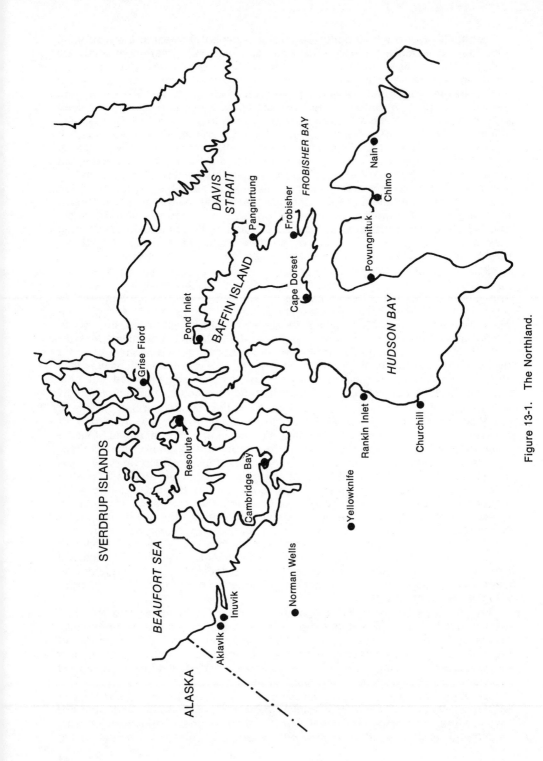

Figure 13-1. The Northland.

SVERDRUP ISLANDS

BEAUFORT SEA

ALASKA

Aklavik
Inuvik

Norman Wells

Grise Fiord

Resolute

Cambridge Bay

Pond Inlet

BAFFIN ISLAND

DAVIS STRAIT

Pangnirtung

Frobisher

FROBISHER BAY

Cape Dorset

Yellowknife

Rankin Inlet

Churchill

HUDSON BAY

Povungnituk

Chimo

Nain

by making and selling works of art. Pangnirtung and Povungnituk have also become important art centres, selling carvings all over the world through the use of Eskimo co-operatives. Co-operatives have also been developed for the catching and marketing of Arctic char (e.g., the West Baffin Eskimo Co-operative sells char to Toronto and Montreal markets), and for the owning and supervision of hunting lodges established for southerners who want to hunt northern-style with Eskimo guides. The tourist trade as a whole is only just beginning to grow and possibly represents the next major wave of development. After all, the countryside is now emptier of people than it probably ever has been before, and the wilderness is certainly there for people to come and experience.

If the tourist trade is not the development leader, then it will almost certainly take second place only to mining. Oil and gas in particular are likely major sources of development, not only in the Mackenzie region but also on the far-north islands. But whatever happens, the process of change in the Northland is by no means finished. You could almost say that it has only just begun.

13-1. There are many (many, many) factors hindering economic development in the Northland. What are some of them, do you think?

13-2. The following list contains a selection of key words in the development of the Northland. Re-arrange them into chronological order according to the text in this study, and write a short explanatory note for each of them.

musk-oxen	Grise Fiord	RCMP
radar	polar bears	co-operatives
radio	missiles	whalers
reindeer	Franklin	Eskimo prints
tourists	weather stations	mining
foxes	lodges	bushplanes
railway	oil and gas	Frobisher
seals	staging posts	Americans
Sverdrup	carvings	tourists
wilderness	re-settlement	disease

13-3. Throughout the Northland today there are about 20 000 Eskimos and Indians, mostly Eskimos. Half of these are children, because the birth rate in the Northland is one of the highest in the world. About 10% of the remainder are too old to work properly, even though the death rate is high and life expectancy in general short (life expectancy for Eskimos and Indians is about 40 years compared with about 73 for Euro-Canadians, as most of the rest of us are called in distinction to the "native peoples"). About 40% of the remainder are women, who are not only outnumbered by men but also greatly out-employed. The women traditionally stay at home, and this is probably going to be one of the last things to change in the North. Calculate the likely maximum local native labour force in the Northland, and draw a divided circle graph[5] to illustrate the above-mentioned population break-down. Do you want to add anything to your answer to 13-1?

A northern bush plane.

13-4. Gigantic projects are planned for the Northland, such as the Mackenzie Valley Pipeline and the James Bay Hydro Project, and vast amounts of detailed analysis have been produced. The Canadian Arctic Gas Study has made extraordinarily thorough investigations into the possible effects of gas exploitation on the natural environment. The federally sponsored Great Plains Project has analyzed and investigated. And we still lack precise data. Many things about the Northland are still not even known about, let alone quantified. This study is therefore different from many of our others: it lacks a statistical basis. Can you suggest why?

If you're really interested in the Northland you should get hold of the following magazine articles from your library:

Eskimos of Grise Fiord, by Fred Bruemmer, *Canadian Geographical Journal,* 1968

Pushing back the Northern Frontier, by Margaret Macdonald, Harry Walker and Gillian Godfrey, *Canadian Geographical Journal,* 1968

The Mackenzie Delta, by J. Ross Mackay, *Canadian Geographical Journal,* 1969

Two Communities in the Eastern Arctic, by Courtney Bond, *Canadian Geographical Journal,* 1970

The Canadian Northwest, by William Wonders, *Canadian Geographical Journal,* 1970

Growing up in Canada's Frozen North, by Eva Fry, *Geographical Magazine,* 1969

Three Life-styles for Ungava Eskimos, by David Riches, *Geographical Magazine,* 1973.

And perhaps also try to see the movie made for HBC's tercentenary in 1970, *Merchants in a Changing Land.*

14 Pollution

MAN THE CHOOSER

The poet R. B. Weedon once wrote, "The world needs a place where wolves stalk the strand lines in the dark, because a land which can produce a wolf is a healthy, robust, and perfect land."

It is an irony that several areas in Canada still have bounties on the wolf. We all want Canada to be healthy, robust, and perfect yet there are many signs that all is not well with our animals, fish, birds, plants, air, water, and land. The effects of pollution are to be seen in all of these media. Worse yet, all is not well with the Canadian people. Many people die each year from afflictions either caused or aggravated by the effects of pollution on the human body. Worst of all, it is ourselves we have to blame for this. People cause pollution. Let us embark on a pollution tour of Canada. It will set the mood for the rest of this study unit.

Placentia Bay, Newfoundland. The ERCO chemical plant there dumped elemental phosphorus into the sea and ruined the livelihood of the fishermen. Inland paper mills, municipal sewage, and tailing heaps beside copper and zinc mines send noxious chemicals into the freshwater streams of the Province.

New Brunswick's problems are similar and include the careless use of agricultural chemicals, chiefly pesticides.

Human sewage has closed the shellfish beds in some areas of Prince Edward Island.

Quebec leads Canada in the lack of municipal sewage treatment. More than 90 percent of Montreal's sewage goes untreated into the St. Lawrence.

Ontario — the most heavily industrialized province — comes out fairly well but when did you last enjoy a glass of Toronto harbour water?

The agricultural prairies use great quantities of fertilizer and pesticide. These persistent chemicals either cause algal blooms in lakes or result in the sterility and death of species of animals which are at the end of food chains, e.g., peregrine falcons and fish.

British Columbia suffers from paper mill pollution, the non-treatment of sewage, and the widespread use of fertilizer and pesticides.

Even the north does not escape. Whitehorse has permitted human sewage to pollute the Yukon River. Yellowknife's water supply was laced with arsenic for a while; it derived from the wastes of gold mines. Anyway, it was easy to cure. They just changed the source of the town's water supply.

Eskimos living off caribou have radiation levels ten times those of their southern fellow-countrymen. The caribou eat quantities of a lichen with an unparalleled ability to absorb and concentrate radio-active fallout from nuclear tests.

But enough. It is not the purpose of this study to make you gag, but rather to say that since each and every one of us lives and consumes according to the dictates of twentieth century technology then each and every one of us must shoulder some of the responsibility for pollution.

The food we eat is fertilized and treated for pests. The cars we drive add unburnt hydrocarbons to the atmosphere. Our airplanes put dust, gases, and water vapour high into the stratosphere, increasing cloud and reducing the amount of radiation coming from the sun. Paints and plastics use a family of chemicals called PCBs which tend to resist biodegradation. Noise in cities contributes to human psychological disorders. Thermal power stations put gases into the atmosphere and thermally pollute streams and lakes with their cooling water. Phosphates and other nutrients from sewage and fertilizers encourage blooms of algae in ponds and lakes. These quickly use up dissolved oxygen in the water, and many forms of aquatic life become menaced. It is possible to continue spelling out the ways in which we all participate in the pollution of our environment but we do not have enough space to do that. Nor do we have enough space to deal with any more than one form of pollution.

What is the extent to which the average Canadian pollutes the air? One man who asked it recently was E. R. Mitchell of the Department of Mines, Energy and Natural Resources in Ottawa, but he did not find it easy to answer. He could not find any facts and figures to help him so he decided to monitor his family for one year and keep a check on their pollution potential. He published his results in May 1971 and some of them are in Figure 14-1.

	Oxygen used	Carbon dioxide produced tonnes per year	Harmful pollutants produced
Gasoline consumption in I/C engines	3.0	2.7	
Combustion of fuel oil in homes	2.7	2.5	
Thermal electricity generation	1.1	1.3	data
			not
Services: the direct and indirect consumption of diesel, aviation and other fuels	8.2	7.9	available
Breathing	0.2	0.7	
Total	17.2	15.1	1.1

Figure 14-1.   The personal pollution inventory of an average Canadian, 1970.

E. R. Mitchell is fairly typical of many Canadians. He drives a car, uses industrial products, puts out garbage and trash, uses electricity, and breathes. We are going to use Mr. Mitchell as a surrogate for the average Canadian in order to develop some ideas.

14-1.   Draw a sketch of an average Canadian!?! By means of coloured, proportional arrows[11] show the data in Figure 14-1. For example, you might colour the oxygen arrows in red. Just be sure to have the arrows pointing the correct ways.

Okay. So we use up oxygen and "fix" some of it as carbon dioxide. So what? People have been doing that for thousands of years, and we aren't running out of the gas. That is true, but we have never used so much as we do today, and, furthermore, our rate of use of oxygen is accelerating. Today we fix more oxygen in carbon dioxide than our northern forests can cope with. They take in carbon dioxide during photosynthesis and release oxygen. The snag is, these great northern forests are dormant for half the year. We therefore rely on more than our fair share of the phyto-plankton in the world's oceans to unlock the oxygen.

The reason why we are worried about the increasing concentration of carbon dioxide in the atmosphere is that this gas gives a "greenhouse" effect to the sun's rays. It absorbs heat but doesn't radiate it very well. It has a tendency to warm up the atmosphere. And that could have ultimately fatal consequences, couldn't it?

Source of air pollution	Total quantity	Carbon dioxide	Harmful pollutants: NO, CO, SO_2, SO_3, dust particles
		million tonnes	
Domestic fuels	58.3	57.9	0.4
Commercial fuels (diesel fuel etc.)	91.2	74.1	17.1
Industrial fuel combustion	136.4	134.7	1.7
Other fuels (smelting, cement and lime works)	13.6	9.1	4.5
Total	299.5	275.8	23.7

Figure 14-2.   The chief sources of air pollution — fuel combustion, 1971.

14-2.   Construct two divided circles[5] to show the data in Figure 14-2. Each circle's area will represent the total amount of air pollution. Divide one circle to show the contributions by each fuel source. Divide the other circle to show the kind of pollution created (carbon dioxide and harmful pollutants).

Assume carbon dioxide is not injurious to man directly. Which source of air pollution puts out proportionately the lowest quantity of harmful pollutants? Does the answer surprise you? How do the other air pollution sources compare? That is, for each ton of air pollution caused by each of the four sources, how much is harmful?

As you are now well aware, the largest air pollutant by weight is carbon dioxide. We assume that it is not directly harmful to man in anything like its present concentration, but we cannot be absolutely sure.

Even the list of harmful pollutants in the table for Figure 14-2 is probably incomplete. And it is a fair assumption that we do not even know all the ways that the known harmful pollutants affect us. We are in a state of relative ignorance here, and it can be only remedied with a lot of research.

If you recall, we said earlier that people pollute. It seems reasonable therefore that we should find the highest levels of air pollution wherever we find the greatest densities of population. Perhaps you realize that this means the cities of Canada should be the most heavily air polluted. Seventy-six percent of Canada's people live in cities and most of these cities are found within 500 km of the U.S. border.

It has been estimated that 60 percent of Canada's 22 million people live in only 2.5 percent of Canada's 10 million sq. km. This is in the highly industrialized and urbanized Great Lakes-St. Lawrence lowlands region.

14-3.   Calculate Canada's overall population density and the density of population along the Great Lakes-St. Lawrence region.

Now look at Figure 14-1 again. Calculate the average amount of air pollution (carbon dioxide and harmful pollutants combined) for a sq. km for one year in

    i) all of Canada
    Ii) the Great Lakes-St. Lawrence region.

How much is that in each of these sq. km in a day?

Fine. Yet the St. Lawrence valley and the shores of the Great Lakes are not carpeted completely with cities. In fact, these people "clusters" are separated by relatively open stretches of countryside. Most of Canada's cities have this in common: there is an old, urban core at the centre of each city. Often referred to as the downtown, population densities here are higher than elsewhere in the city — in the suburban fringe, for example. In addition, cities of any size tend to have their own climatic "lid" on pollution which prevents it escaping freely. Right at the city centre, then, is where we would expect to find most of the highest air pollution levels in Canada. Agreed?

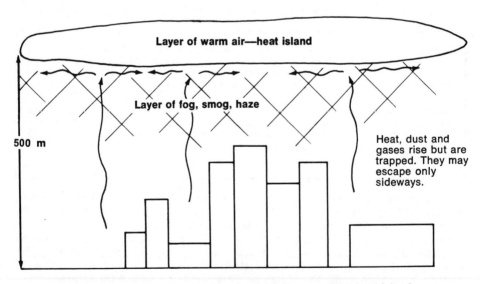

Figure 14-3.   The climate of a city: the influence of the heat island.

City	Population	Area (sq. km)
Toronto	712 786	97
St. John's	88 102	31
St. John	89 039	323
Saskatoon	126 449	95
Sudbury	90 535	121
Thunder Bay	108 411	323
Vancouver	426 256	113
Winnipeg	246 246	79
Calgary	403 319	404
Edmonton	438 152	281
Halifax	122 035	63
Hamilton	309 173	123
Kitchener	111 804	67
London	223 222	160
Montreal	214 352	158
Ottawa/Hull	365 921	137
Quebec	186 088	71
Regina	139 469	76
St. Catharines	109 722	94
Windsor	203 300	120
Victoria	61 761	19
Chicoutimi	33 893	29

Figure 14-4.   The cities of Canada, 1971.

14-4. On a map of Canada, represent each of the cities listed in Figure 14-4 by means of a circle about the size of a dime.

Now. In our present state of ignorance it is suggested that depending on the amount of industry there is in a city, population densities should never be allowed above 3 860 people per sq. km and that, ideally, there should never be more than 1 544 people per sq. km. Calculate the densities of population in each of the cities you have located on your map. Devise a colour scheme[11] and a legend to show if a city has exceeded the danger limit, if it has exceeded the ideal limit, or whether the city still has "room to breathe."

By way of a conclusion, we will make a decision concerning Canada's future. The total inhabited area of Canada is some 420 000 sq. km. Of that, assume that we will only ever want 3 percent of it to be covered with cities. (The present figure is 2.5 percent.) Using the critical population densities given in assignment 14-4 try this:

14-5. If the maximum permissible city population densities were allowed, what would be the size of Canada's urban population? The total population (assuming 80 percent of it was urban)?

Calculate the equivalent figures for ideal city population densities.

A word of caution. Air pollution is an unwelcome product of modern technology. It represents (mainly) accumulations of combustion products that aroused little concern until recently. Imagine that industry could trap and sell profitably these "waste" gases and dust particles. Suppose that electric cars become acceptable and economical to produce and run. How valid are your answers to 14-5 then? We have the technology to curb air pollution now. The big decision we shall have to make soon is not whether we can afford to reduce air pollution but whether we can afford not to.

15 Ports and Trade

SPATIAL INTERACTION

Ports are the doorways in and out of a region. They may have international traffic passing through, or they may have merely local traffic passing through. Either way, they are the points where a region has contact with other areas. This contact may be in the form of freight, whereby the products of one country move into another area to be used, or it may be in the form of people, who may visit, come on business, or even immigrate.

Canada has a lot of ports, because it is such a large country. Some of them serve just local areas, while others serve overseas areas as well. In addition, some of them (such as Edmonton) serve only air traffic, while others (such as Montreal) serve both air and sea traffic.

	Cargo tonnes: international traffic	Cargo tonnes: coastal traffic	Cargo tonnes: total traffic	s.r.
Vancouver	13 343 195	11 018 530	24 361 725	4896
Sept-Iles	15 716 559	3 691 601	19 408 160	4370
Montreal	9 377 288	8 608 191	17 985 479	4215
Thunder Bay	3 540 320	10 578 067	14 118 387	3727
Port Cartier	11 715 998	784 464	12 500 462	3507
Hamilton	7 229 644	4 067 676	11 297 320	3334
Halifax	7 775 636	2 754 022	10 529 658	3218
Quebec	4 110 676	3 300 578	7 411 254	2701
Toronto	4 252 654	2 249 390	6 502 044	2530
St. John	4 569 037	1 667 374	6 236 411	2478

Figure 15-1. Seaport data, *Canada Yearbook, 1972.*

15-1. Using the data in Figure 15-1, draw proportional circles[4] on a large map of Canada to show the relative importance of the ten chief seaports. Divide the circles[5] according to the proportions of international and local (coastal) traffic. Can you suggest any explanations for the traffic through these ports?

Japanese tanker loading LPG at Vancouver.

	number of itinerant (non-local) flights	s.r.
Toronto	176 611	420
Montreal	152 342	389
Vancouver	132 606	363
Winnipeg	117 949	342
Ottawa	89 169	298

Figure 15-2. Airport data, *Canada Yearbook, 1972.*

15-2. Figure 15-2 gives information about the number of non-local flights in and out of Canada's five major airports. Plot the information as proportional circles[4] on a map of Canada; then suggest why the top five airports in Canada are not the same as the first five seaports.

We have now identified and located the major gateways of Canada. What we should do next is try to obtain a generalized idea of how these ports serve to link Canada to the rest of the world.

	Halifax	St. John	Montreal	Quebec
Britain	522 525	348 395	1 290 572	561 267
Continental Europe	391 225	507 931	2 880 128	1 844 658
Middle East	172 559	3 032 921	294 115	522 103
Africa	26 365	173 735	955 139	25 357
Asia	88 469	108 544	574 145	298 053
Oceania	50 554	352 003	195 225	59 734
South America	3 752 872	753 123	828 948	1 249 151
Central America & West Indies	796 783	386 446	1 430 644	630 164
U.S.A.	1 897 182	219 701	1 454 335	735 174

	Hamilton	Thunder Bay	Toronto	Vancouver
Britain	101 973	237 849	114 052	406 977
Continental Europe	118 408	943 854	235 540	1 695 444
Middle East	6 437	16 701	2 177	207 103
Africa	7 244	24 490	51 936	33 904
Asia	25 774	33 723	241 574	15 188 054
Oceania	8 809	—	11 800	784 411
South America	35 562	7 460	46 616	502 197
Central America & West Indies	66 232	43 911	125 827	385 610
U.S.A.	5 001 961	2 444 831	1 377 673	3 282 862

Figure 15-3. Total sea-borne trade, in tonnes, *Statistics Canada, 1973.*

15-3. The generalized world trade of eight of Canada's busiest ten seaports (excluding the two highly specialized ports of Sept-Iles and Port Cartier) is shown in Figure 15-3. On a *large* map of the world, drawn (or cut-and-pasted) so that the Americas are in the centre, draw bright lines to connect each of the ports in Canada with all the parts of the world that it trades with. You probably won't be able to use proportional-width arrows because your map won't be big enough, but if you get a really big map then it would be a good idea to use proportional-width arrows.[11]

It is pretty clear now that Canada's links around the world just through trade are very wide-ranging. However, let's have a closer look at just one port and see how it has links with the rest of the world.

Britain*	Ivory Coast	Cuba*
Belgium*	Liberia	Dominican Rep.
Denmark	Mozambique	Guatemala
Finland	Senegal	Haiti
France	Spanish Africa	Honduras
West Germany*	Togo	Mexico
Greece	Ceylon (Sri Lanka)	Aruba*
Iceland	Hong Kong	Curacao
Ireland	India	Panama
Italy*	Malaysia	Puerto Rico
Netherlands*	Pakistan	Greenland
Norway	Singapore	St. Pierre & Miquelon*
Portugal	Indonesia	U.S.A.:
Spain	Japan*	Chicago
Sweden*	Korea (South)	Cleveland
Switzerland	Phillipines	Baltimore*
U.S.S.R.	Taiwan	Boston
Israel	Thailand	Burlington*
Kuwait	Australia*	Edgewater*
Lebanon	New Zealand	Jacksonville*
Saudi Arabia*	Guyana	New Haven*
Syria	Argentina	New Orleans
Turkey*	Brazil	New York*
U.A.R. (Egypt)	Chile	Portsmouth*
Ghana	Colombia*	Savannah*
Kenya	Ecuador	Tampa*
Nigeria	Peru	Wilmington*
South African Rep.	Venezuela*	Houston*
Sierra Leone	Bahamas*	*indicates a total trade
Algeria	Bermuda	exceeding 20 000 tonnes.
Angola	Br. Honduras	
Cameroun	Barbados	
Dahomey	Jamaica*	
French Africa	Leeward Isles	
Gabon	Trinidad & Tobago*	
Guinea	Windward Isles	

Figure 15-4.   List of places served by Halifax, *Statistics Canada, 1973.*

15-4.   Using the information in Figure 15-4 and a large world map, draw lines from Halifax to all the places listed. Make the lines to those places which have a total trade with Halifax of more than 20 000 tonnes a brighter colour than the rest of the lines. Whereabouts in the world are most of the countries that do no trade at all with Halifax?

If, instead of taking the links through one port, we take the links for one product, we find that Canada's interaction with other parts of the world is still pretty impressive. Wheat is, of course, one of Canada's major exports, but it nevertheless illustrates vividly how Canada depends on the rest of the world.

	tonnes	s.r.		tonnes	s.r.
Halifax	378 216	615	Trois Rivieres	574 769	758
St. John	427 997	654	Sarnia	5 457	74
Bale Comeau	1 398 452	1182	Thunder Bay	118 517	344
Montreal	1 826 498	1351	Churchill	513 406	717
Port Cartier	1 284 416	1133	Prince Rupert	354 693	595
Quebec	581 800	763	Vancouver	5 235 497	2288
Sorel	620 551	788	Victoria	166 426	408

Destinations of shipments from:

Montreal		Vancouver
Britain	India	Britain
Malta	Pakistan	Belgium
Belgium	Indonesia	West Germany
France	Argentina	Netherlands
West Germany	Brazil	Iraq
Greece	Venezuela	Saudi Arabia
Ireland	Barbados	South African Rep.
Italy	Cuba	Hong Kong
Netherlands	Dominican Rep.	India
Norway	Haiti	Malaysia
Portugal		Pakistan
Albania		Singapore
Poland		China
U.S.S.R.		Japan
Iraq		North Korea
Lebanon		South Korea
Syria		Phillipines
U.A.R. (Egypt)		Taiwan
Ghana		Thailand
Nigeria		U.S.S.R.
Algeria		Ecuador
Morocco		Peru
Tunisia		Venezuela

Figure 15-5.   Wheat export data, *Statistics Canada, 1973.*

15-5.   Figure 15-5 gives information for the wheat ports of Canada. Use the s.r. numbers to draw proportional circles[4] on a map of Canada to represent the wheat trade through these ports. Then obtain a world map and on it draw lines from (a) Vancouver and (b) Montreal to all the places around the world that Vancouver and Montreal send shipments of wheat to. Use two different bright colours.

15-6.   We just noted that Canada's wheat exports show how Canada depends on the rest of the world. Shouldn't that be . . . show how the rest of the world depends on Canada? What do you think? Put your hand up after you've thought about it a while.

Finally, let's take a little look at how different places are linked together just within Canada. We can do this very simply by looking at the information in Figure 15-6 and plotting it on a map of Canada . . .

Newfoundland and Labrador	Gaspe	Cornwall
Corner Brook	Grindstone	Goderich
Goose Bay	Havre St. Pierre	Hamilton
Harbour Grace	Matane	Kingston
Holyrood	Mont Louis	Marathon
Lewisporte	Contrecoeur	Morrisburg
Long Pond	Lanoraie	Oakville
St. Johns	Varennes	Oshawa
Stephenville	Point au Pic	Owen Sound
Maritimes	Port Cartier	Port Colborne
Charlottetown	Port Menier	Port Credit
Halifax	Quebec	Port Stanley
Little Narrows	Rimouski	Prescott
Port Hawkesbury	Riviere du Loup	Sault Ste. Marie
Pugwash	Sept Iles	Thorold
Sydney	Ste. Anne des Monts	Thunder Bay
Bathurst	Sorel	Toronto
Chatham	Trois Rivieres	Welland
Dalhousie	Ontario	Windsor
Newcastle	Amherstburg	Manitoba
Quebec	Belleville	Churchill
Baie Comeau	Clarkson	Northwest Territories
Chicoutimi	Cobourg	Frobisher Bay
Forestville	Collingwood	

Figure 15-6.   A list of places served by coastal shipping to and from Montreal, as an example of domestic shipping links, from *Statistics Canada, 1973.*

15-7.   On a map of Canada put bold red dots at all the locations shown in Figure 15-6. The title of your map is . . . well, it's whatever will tell a stranger what the map is about; so make sure you've got a good title.

---

16 The Prairies

AREAL DIFFERENTIATION

Did you know that there are some parts of the Prairies where a farmer can go bankrupt if he tries to grow wheat? Hundreds of farmers have found that out, to their sorrow, and many have just given up and left the Prairies altogether.

Did you know that about a mile or so beneath the Prairie sod there are the remains of age-old coral reefs? The oil-men do, because that's where they find much of their oil.

Did you know that the Albertans can produce sulfur so cheaply that they have the American sulfur producers gnashing their teeth? Or that the biggest potash mines in the world are in Saskatchewan? Or that dinosaurs used to roam the lands of Alberta? Or that the word Winnipeg means murky waters?

There's probably a lot of things you don't know about the Prairies. Let's just see.

They are not flat, for a start. Parts of them are, of course; but parts of them aren't, either. In the east, around Winnipeg, you have the lowest parts: heights are about 200 metres, and the land is quite flat. Indeed, much of the land around Winnipeg used to be the muddy bottom of a great lake after the glaciers had started to melt. The silty deposits are now flat and fertile. By the way, can you see the origin of "murky waters"? As you go westwards, you cross out of the Winnipeg lowlands and start to face a belt of higher land.

The early settlers called this belt of higher land *mountains*, because it looked so high after they had crossed the Winnipeg lowlands. The different parts were called different names (such as Riding Mountain and Duck Mountain), but the whole thing was called the Manitoba Escarpment. As you go still farther west, halfway across Saskatchewan you come to another range of hills. This was called the Missouri Coteau by the early French voyageurs (who were they?). After crossing the Coteau, you then come to a part of the Prairies which is anything but flat. The land rolls, steepens, flattens out, and rolls again. Hills rise out above the general rolling ground, and steep-sided valleys are cut by large rivers into the rolling ground. You are now coming to Alberta.

In Alberta the Prairies rise up to the foothills of the Rockies. The height of the western Prairies is about 1500 metres, which is quite a bit different from the 200 metres of the Winnipeg lowlands; along the way you have had two major escarpments and an assortment of minor and major hills. So you can't think of the Prairies any longer as having the same sort of topography all over.

How about climate then? Surely the climate is pretty much the same throughout the Prairies? Well, it's certainly *similar*, but it's not all the *same*. The greatest degree of sameness occurs with the summer temperatures, which average around 17-19°C throughout the entire Prairie region. Winter temperatures vary considerably more: from about −10°C near the extreme south-west of Alberta to about −20°C near Lake Winnipeg. In general, winter temperatures drop from the Rockies to Hudson Bay. But they are all cold. The chief differentiating factor is the Chinook, which is felt in south-western Alberta mostly. The Chinook is a warm drying wind which comes down from the Rockies in winter and spring (it may come in summer and fall as well, but you wouldn't notice its warming effect then; so it's really a winter and spring phenomenon). The warming effects of the Chinook are usually felt in the Calgary-Lethbridge-Medicine Hat district, but they may at times spread farther east into Saskatchewan. Let's see how it works. In Figure 16-1 you can see a moisture-bearing wind approaching the western side of the Rockies (and if you've been on the western side of the Rockies you will remember just how moisture-bearing those winds can be!). When this wind reaches the Rockies it has to rise to go over them. It then cools. The rate at which it cools is called the saturated adiabatic lapse rate, and it is about 5°C/1000 metres. This means that if a wind has a temperature of 8°C when it starts up the western side of the mountains then it will have a temperaure of −7°C when it has climbed up 3000 metres.

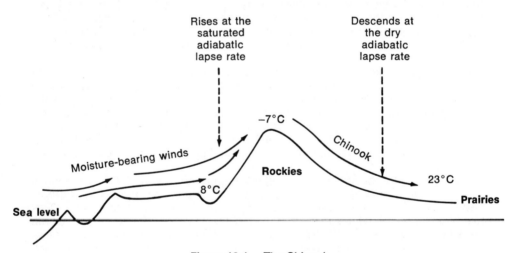

Figure 16-1. The Chinook.

When the wind comes down the eastern side to the Prairies, however, it gets warmer (because of the pressure of increasingly more air above it); it gets warmer at what is called the dry adiabatic lapse rate, which is about 10°C/1000 metres. The Chinook, as it is now called when it comes down, gains a temperature of 30°C when it descends 3000 metres. Since its temperature when it crossed the mountains was −7°C, then its temperature when it gets down the Prairies is 23°C. This is quite a warm spell for a Prairie winter or spring day. It doesn't last very long, though.

16-1. Using the lapse rates just described, calculate the Prairie temperatures under the following conditions:

starting temperature	height of mountain	Prairie temperature
20°C	4000 metres	
5°C	2500 metres	
–8°C	2900 metres	

When we turn to precipitation, we find that there are quite large differences between the various parts of the Prairies. The southern districts, roughly bounded by a line joining Lethbridge-Red Deer-Saskatoon-Regina-the 49th Parallel – just south of Lethbridge, are almost desert (see Figure 16-2). When this southern region was being surveyed by Palliser back in the nineteenth century, it was described by him as being useless for settlement. The area is now known as Palliser's Triangle. And even though it is not exactly useless for settlement, it does support lower population densities than elsewhere in the Prairies. It is also the region where early farmers went bankrupt trying to grow wheat. If you get the chance (ask your teacher), try to see the National Film Board film *The Drylanders*.

Outside Palliser's Triangle, to the north and east, there is more ample rain. Winnipeg, for instance, has almost half as much precipitation again as Saskatoon. And as the quantity of rainfall increases to east and north, so also does its reliability, which means that farmers in the eastern and northern

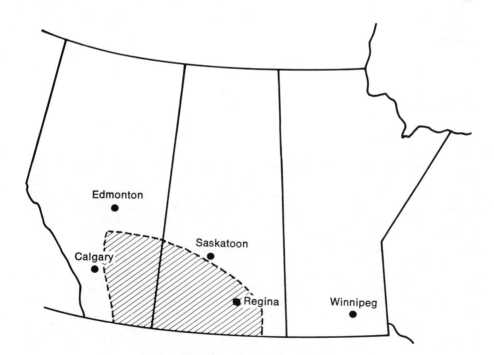

Figure 16-2. Palliser's Triangle.

Prairies can rely on getting enough moisture much more readily than can farmers farther south.

16-2. Enlarge Figure 16-3 on your own paper (or perhaps persuade your teacher to duplicate some already-enlarged copies for you), and isopleth it at 5-centimetre intervals. You will finish up with a detailed precipitation map of the Prairies and a good idea of the areal variations within the Prairies (we hope).

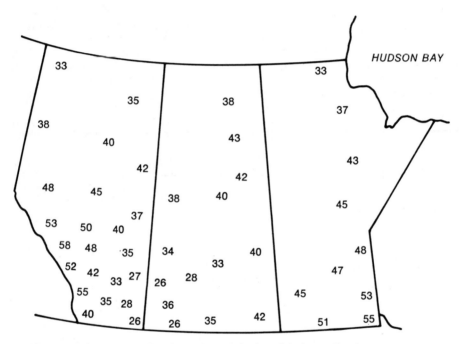

Figure 16-3. Annual precipitation data in centimetres.

Plants can also rely on getting sufficient moisture around the outer edges of the Prairies as well. In the inner heart — Palliser's Triangle — only hardy grasses grow naturally, while towards the edges, as precipitation becomes greater and more reliable, you find some trees (such as aspen and poplar) as well as grass. This outer region is known as the Parkland Belt. It runs approximately from Winnipeg to the north of Saskatoon and then to Edmonton and on down the foothills of the Rockies past Calgary.

Because the natural vegetation varies with the precipitation in this way, so also do the soils. In the Parkland Belt the soils are rich and black; they are called *chernozem* soils. But in the grassy semi-desert of Palliser's Triangle the soils are only brown and moderately fertile; they are called *brown* soils. Why aren't they so fertile? Well, when grass decays in the soil it does not form as much humus as when trees decay in the soil, so you get the richer soils where you get some trees decaying as well. Why don't you get the most fertile soils in the forest belt to the north then?

You answer that one.

With all the differences in topography, temperature, precipitation, vegetation, and soils that we've just looked at, you'd be quite right in assuming that there are differences in farming as well. Everyone knows wheat is important, but it's certainly not important everywhere. The best lands for wheat are the chernozem soils in the Parkland Belt, but unfortunately for wheat they are also the best lands for many other types of farming. Competition for space therefore keeps the wheat plantings down here, forcing the main wheat-lands to exist in the edges of Palliser's Triangle, where conditions are too dry for most other crops. Saskatchewan has the greatest quantity of land in Palliser's Triangle (Figure 16-2), and it therefore has the largest amount of land under wheat. Alberta, of course, ranks second, followed by Manitoba.

	average 1960-70 number of hectares under wheat
Prince Edward Island	1 215 000
Nova Scotia	405 000
New Brunswick	1 215 000
Quebec	9 315 000
Ontario	168 885 000
Manitoba	1 340 995 000
Saskatchewan	7 669 485 000
Alberta	2 540 565 000
British Columbia	44 145 000

Figure 16-4.   Land under wheat, by provinces.

16-3.   Construct a divided circle graph[5] to illustrate the variations between the different provinces in the amount of land under wheat, according to the data in Figure 16-4.

The very driest parts of Palliser's Triangle, between Calgary and Swift Current, are too dry for even wheat. Instead they are used for grazing cattle. And again, Alberta and Saskatchewan greatly outweigh Manitoba in importance.

	Alberta	Saskatchewan	Manitoba
Horses	80 000	65 000	30 000
Cattle	3 535 000	2 386 000	1 120 000
Sheep	247 000	126 000	47 000
Pigs	1 600 000	985 000	884 000

Figure 16-5.   Numbers of livestock in the Prairies, 1970.

16-4.   Construct a series of overlapping bars[17] to illustrate the pattern of live-stock distribution in the three Prairie provinces.

Manitoba, which is the wettest and most fertile part of the Prairies (don't forget the chernozem soils and the lake-bed soils), is noted more for the mixture of farm products than for any single product. In the districts south of Winnipeg it is possible to grow many vegetables, and even some sugar

Oil, wheat, and rough-land in Alberta.

beet, which is difficult to grow elsewhere in the Prairies. There is also a more intensive dairying industry, and there is even some corn grown (and that really is unusual in the Prairies). The only part of the Prairies to rival the variety of the Winnipeg region is the district around Lethbridge, where the ready availability of irrigation water together with the periodic warming effect of the Chinook winds combine to allow vegetables and sugar beet to be grown.

If we turn from farming to minerals, we find that differences which exist on the surface still persist underground. Alberta, for example, has more than twice the value of mineral production as the two other Prairie provinces together, even though most of this value is oil and gas. Saskatchewan and Manitoba are roughly equal to each other in value of mineral output, but the minerals are greatly different. Saskatchewan produces mainly potash and petroleum, while Manitoba produces chiefly nickel and copper (in the Shield part of the province rather than in the Prairie part proper). In broad terms, the minerals produced by Alberta and Saskatchewan are very similar, and quite different from those produced in Manitoba.

	Alberta	all values in $ Saskatchewan	Manitoba
Coal	25 656 000	7 299 000	—
Natural gas	453 242 000	11 152 000	—
Petroleum	845 270 000	201 163 000	16 307 000
Nickel	—	—	212 649 000
Copper	—	18 058 000	59 748 000
Zinc	—	6 740 000	12 593 000
Other metals	2 000	12 371 000	8 702 000
Potash	—	116 402 000	—
Salt	2 039 000	3 358 000	185 000
Others	67 294 000	15 964 000	23 078 000
TOTAL VALUES	1 393 503 000	392 507 000	333 262 000

Figure 16-6. Mineral production data, 1970 values in $.

16-5. Draw three percentage bar graphs[3] to bring out the differences between the three Prairie provinces, using the mineral data in Figure 16-6.

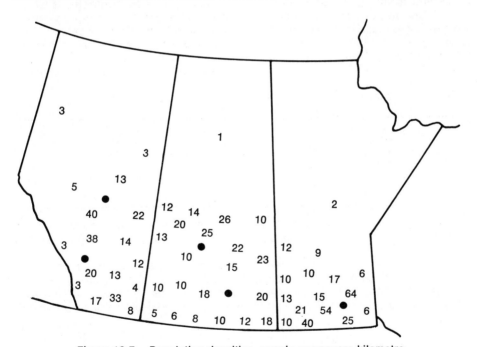

Figure 16-7. Population densities, people per square kilometre.

16-6. Obtain an enlarged copy of Figure 16-7. It shows a variety of population densities scattered over the Prairies. Your job is to isopleth the map, which shouldn't be too difficult a task if you've understood everything so far! Go to it.

17 Land Use in Southern Ontario

AREAL DIFFERENTIATION

Where is Southern Ontario? Approximately one third of Canada's people call it home without really knowing its precise limits (it ends up north somewhere!). For the purposes of this study unit, Southern Ontario is made up of the counties shown in Figure 17-1.

Within the area of Southern Ontario lies a great deal of land. To say that it occupies 11.6 percent of the land area of Ontario or only 1.2 percent of all Canada's land area belies its true importance. Much of Canada's most fertile and productive land lies in these counties, several of Canada's largest cities and towns, and a very great deal of Canada's manufacturing industry.

With an area of some 10.5 million hectares, Southern Ontario is larger than Belgium, Austria, Denmark, or Hungary. Its population was revealed to be 6 896 557 by the 1971 census — higher than that of many other countries including Norway, Switzerland, Jordan, and Syria.

It is the uses to which the land area of Southern Ontario is put that concern us. Accordingly, we might try and establish just how much land each person in Southern Ontario would have if it were all shared out equally.

17-1. In all of Canada there are some 997 614 000 hectares on which exists a population of perhaps 22 million people. How many hectares does each person have to support himself? (or herself?) What is the corresponding figure for an inhabitant of Southern Ontario? Show your answers as proportional squares drawn beside each other with the distance of one side of each square given in metres.

In view of assignment 17-1 then, we might pose the question of how so many people are able to live in Southern Ontario and enjoy a high standard of living.

So far as man is concerned, land may only be used in two ways: for working and for pleasure. Let us look at the work aspect first, bearing in mind that people tend to live near their work. If we can find out where most people live, then we shall have found out where most jobs are to be found. Correct?

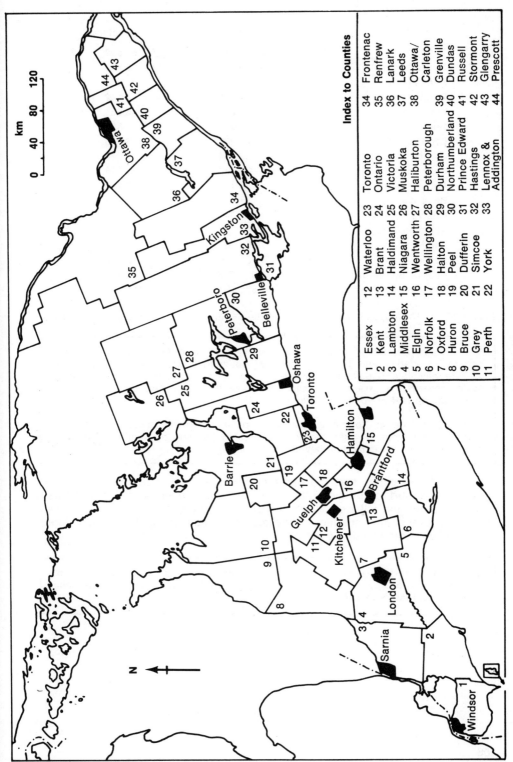

Index to Counties

1	Essex	12	Waterloo	23	Toronto	34	Frontenac
2	Kent	13	Brant	24	Ontario	35	Renfrew
3	Lambton	14	Haldimand	25	Victoria	36	Lanark
4	Middlesex	15	Niagara	26	Muskoka	37	Leeds
5	Elgin	16	Wentworth	27	Haliburton	38	Ottawa/ Carleton
6	Norfolk	17	Wellington	28	Peterborough	39	Grenville
7	Oxford	18	Halton	29	Durham	40	Dundas
8	Huron	19	Peel	30	Northumberland	41	Russell
9	Bruce	20	Dufferin	31	Prince Edward	42	Stormont
10	Grey	21	Simcoe	32	Hastings	43	Glengarry
11	Perth	22	York	33	Lennox & Addington	44	Prescott

Figure 17-1. Southern Ontario.

	Population	Area in hectares
Toronto	2 086 017	55 592
St. Catharines	109 722	9 443
Hamilton	309 173	12 282
Brantford	64 421	4 542
Kitchener	111 804	6 661
Guelph	60 087	6 851
London	223 222	16 045
Sarnia	57 644	3 276
Oshawa	91 587	5 506
Peterborough	58 111	5 299
Belleville	35 128	2 404
Ottawa	302 341	11 015
Kingston	59 047	2 841
Windsor	203 300	11 976
Barrie	27 676	2 896
Rest of Southern Ontario	3 097 277	10 290 554
Total for Southern Ontario	6 896 557	10 447 183

Figure 17-2.   The populations and areas of the major cities of Southern Ontario, 1971.

17-2.   Trace an outline map of Southern Ontario from Figure 17-1. Omit the county boundaries and leave on the city boundaries. Use the data in Figure 17-2 to calculate population densities in people per hectare. Using a suitable scale, construct a raised area map[15] to show the population densities of the cities and the rest of Southern Ontario.

What percentage of Southern Ontario's population lives in those cities? What sort of occupations do they have? Where might the rest of Southern Ontario's people live? Do you think that they are all farmers?

We must remember that the non-city dwellers do not live evenly spread over the land surface outside the major cities. Rather, they are concentrated in small towns and villages. Pretty well the only people living by themselves are farmers and their families. They may be small in numbers but without them, city dwellers couldn't survive.

17-3.   Calculate the length of a side of a square which contains the amount of land that the average city dweller has to support himself. Why do the city dwellers need the farmers?

	average farm size (hectares)	dominant farming type		average farm size (hectares)	dominant farming type
Brant	55	c	Northumberland	72	a
Bruce	83	a	Ontario	62	a
Dufferin	72	a	Ottawa-Carleton	77	b
Dundas	86	b	Oxford	55	b
Durham	62	a	Peel	60	a
Elgin	63	c	Perth	59	a
Essex	38	d	Peterborough	79	a
Frontenac	102	b	Prescott	74	b
Glengarry	76	b	Prince Edward	79	b
Grenville	75	b	Renfrew	110	a
Grey	72	a	Russell	65	b
Haldimand	59	a	Simcoe	63	a
Haliburton	96	a	Stormont	68	b
Halton	47	a	Toronto	25	f
Hastings	92	b	Victoria	87	a
Huron	71	a	Waterloo	51	a
Kent	60	d	Wellington	61	a
Lambton	64	a	Wentworth	37	a
Lanark	114	a	York	49	a
Leeds	94	b			
Lennox & Addington	89	b	Total Ontario		
Middlesex	65	a	average	68	a
Muskoka	87	b			
Niagara	26	e			
Norfolk	48	c			

Note: a = cattle, hogs, and sheep
b = dairying
c = field crops (excl. grains)
d = small grains (excl. wheat)
e = fruits and vegetables
f = specialty farming

Figure 17-3.   The farming of Southern Ontario, 1971.

17-4. Trace another map from Figure 17-1 but this time leave off the cities and mark on only the county boundaries. All counties with a larger-than-average farm size should be shaded black while those counties with a smaller than average farm size should be shaded yellow. There is quite a clear pattern, isn't there? Now staple or glue a sheet of tracing paper to one edge of this map so that it flaps back like the page of a book. Choose a colour to represent the type of farming dominant in each county and shade in this map too (six colours) and then answer these questions:

i) Which type of farming seems to need the largest land areas?

ii) Why is livestock raising not nearly so insistent on large land areas as compared with the farming type mentioned in i)?

iii) Give at least one good reason why crops such as corn, tobacco, and fruits are not scattered very widely throughout Southern Ontario.

17-5. Write one or two paragraphs to explain why Southern Ontario is divided up the way that it is for work. Your answer must include the words *specialization* and *efficiency*.

"All work and no play makes Jack a dull boy!" goes an old proverb. Just like anyone else, the inhabitant of Southern Ontario requires leisure time and leisure space — both land and water. Accordingly, the Ontario government and a few private operators have established parks, conservation areas, canoeing trails, campsites, marinas, motels, hotels, gift shops, museums of the outdoors and nature trails, skiing resorts, snowmobile trails, icefishing huts, and a host of other things to divert, amuse, entertain, and relax.

Private individuals usually aspire to owning a piece of land "up north," usually with water frontage on a lake. Most people buy such land with a view to building a cottage on it.

Recently however, there has been a great upswing in cottage land prices. The Ontario government is not releasing any more Crown land and has laid down stringent rules to guide the development of cottage country. The suitable land available for cottages is thus in short supply at a time when people have never been so mobile, so affluent, or possessed of so much leisure time. And they are demanding the space and facilities for it as Figure 17-4 shows.

Year	Total visitors	Vehicles	Total cash receipts $
1960	5 692 978	1 552 662	568 938
1965	8 875 668	2 437 988	1 335 214
1966	12 172 254	3 468 758	3 082 227

Figure 17-4. The use of Ontario Provincial Parks.

Interestingly enough, a lot of fine cottage land in Southern Ontario was once farmed. This was around the 1900s when free land was granted to pioneers who would settle the more northerly counties in Southern Ontario. Unfortunately this land was marginal; it lay on the edge of the Canadian Shield and was possessed of poor soils and a short growing season because it was farther north. As the profitability of farming decreased, many of these people sold out to others who increased their holdings to maintain a profitable operation. Nowadays farming in these marginal areas doesn't pay nearly as well as selling the land for cottages and recreation.

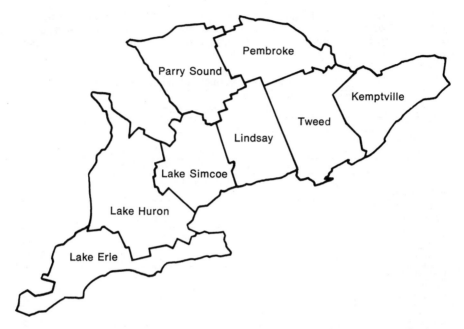

Figure 17-5. Ontario Department of Lands and Forests administrative districts.

Lands and Forests Administrative Districts

Major Occupation	Lake Erie	Lake Huron	Lake Simcoe	Lindsay	Tweed	Kempt-ville	Pem-broke	Parry Sound
Farmer	74.8	75.3	50.8	41.0	43.3	58.4	43.8	19.5
Labourer-Wage earner	5.8	3.8	4.9	10.2	12.6	6.3	11.2	12.3
Clerical-Office	0.9	1.2	1.5	1.3	1.7	2.2	4.5	1.2
Skilled Trades	5.1	3.9	6.2	9.1	9.3	6.5	9.0	15.1
Business-Commercial	2.8	5.3	12.5	11.0	8.9	6.3	14.6	15.5
Professional	2.3	3.5	5.8	9.4	7.5	7.3	2.2	8.4
Housewife-Housekeeper	2.8	2.4	4.2	5.2	3.3	3.1	2.2	6.4
Retired	4.1	3.6	9.3	8.6	11.2	7.3	7.9	13.9
Other	1.3	0.9	4.7	4.2	2.3	2.4	4.5	7.6

Note: Columns may not sum up to 100 percent due to rounding.

Figure 17-6. Landowners' major occupation, 1969, percentage distributions.

A 1969 study by the Ontario Department of Lands and Forests revealed a lot of information about who buys land and why.

109

17-6. Trace a map from Figure 17-5 and colour in black all those districts which had fewer than 50 percent farmers for landowners. This information is obtained from Figure 17-6.

Fine. So now you could guess why so many people other than farmers buy land. They want to use it for recreation probably. If you look at your atlas you could probably say why they choose the areas shaded black in assignment 17-6. Why is that land so popular?

	Lands and Forests Administrative Districts							
Motive	Lake Erie	Lake Huron	Lake Simcoe	Lindsay	Tweed	Kempt-ville	Pem-broke	Parry Sound
Farming	92.9	86.9	69.4	57.4	55.6	73.6	59.4	26.4
Permanent Residence	4.4	4.7	14.1	12.2	14.6	8.6	11.6	18.6
Second Home	—	1.7	6.3	7.7	7.0	5.2	4.3	15.9
Financial Investment	1.8	3.0	4.5	5.8	7.3	5.0	—	8.6
Satisfaction of Land Ownership	2.8	3.4	2.6	4.8	6.3	3.9	8.7	8.2
Satisfaction of Woodland Ownership	1.1	3.2	2.6	3.8	7.8	3.7	13.0	7.7
Commercial Timber Production	—	0.7	0.8	4.2	6.0	2.6	7.2	8.6
Personal Recreation	—	3.1	2.9	9.0	13.6	3.4	8.7	18.2
Commercial Recreation	—	0.5	0.8	2.9	1.8	1.6	—	2.7
Others	1.1	1.1	5.5	3.2	1.3	1.8	2.9	4.5

Note: A dash indicates less than 0.5 percent. Columns may not sum to 100 percent due to owners indicating more than one motive.

Figure 17-7. Land purchase motives, 1969.

The purchase motive for land is very interesting. So far as farming is concerned, it ties in with what we already know about who owns the land. Doesn't it? But look at the other motives. They are a pretty mixed bag, aren't they? Let's simplify it.

17-7. Check through the table given in Figure 17-7 and decide which motives contribute to something called "the personal and recreational purchase motive." Shade in black on a traced outline of Figure 17-5 the four highest scoring districts. Compare this map with the one that you drew for assignment 17-6.

How old do you think most of the people are who buy land for a permanent residence in those four districts? Check back to Figure 17-6 and try to pick out which occupation group these people belong to.

110

A final overview of landowning in Ontario is provided by the data in Figure 17-8.

Distance in km	percentage of owners
Same township	75.5
Within 40	10.7
41-80	3.1
81-250	3.2
251-500	4.4
501-1000	1.4
More than 1000	1.6

Figure 17-8.   The distribution of Southern Ontario landowners by distance from their principal residences, 1969.

17-8.   Construct a cumulative percentage curve[16] to show the data in Figure 17-8. Divide the curve in such a way that farmers are separated from other people. Where do most of the other landowners live?

Recreational activity	Percentage of total recreational activity
Hunting	53.0
Snowmobiling	35.4
Hiking and Walking	27.5
Fishing	17.9
Sleighing and Tobogganing	15.0
Berry picking	13.8
Picnicking	12.9
Trapping	12.0
Swimming	10.9
Horseriding	10.4
Target shooting and Archery	10.2
Skating	9.8
Nature study	8.8
Camping	8.2
Skiing	7.6
Boating	7.4
Others	1.8
No activity	26.6

Figure 17-9.   Use of recreational land in Southern Ontario, 1969.

So much for the people who own land in Southern Ontario. Figure 17-9 shows you that it is not necessary to own a piece of land in order to enjoy a recreational activity. On the contrary, you could enjoy the land as a tourist who stays in the region for only a few weeks.

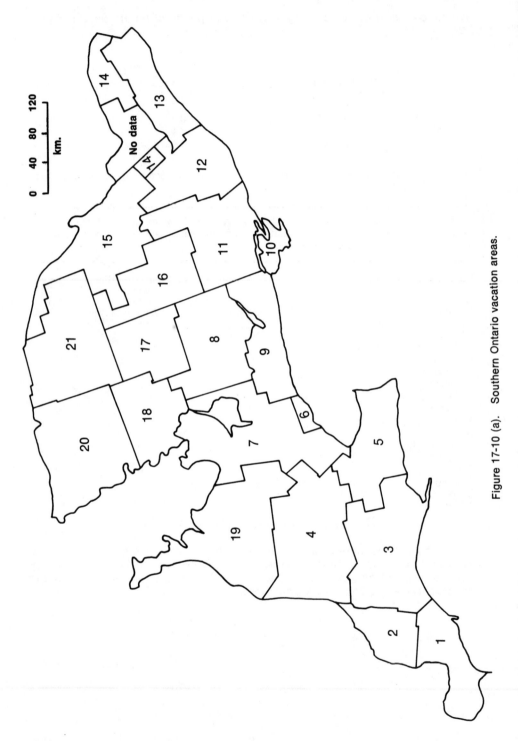

Figure 17-10 (a). Southern Ontario vacation areas.

Vacation area	Percentage of visitors
1. Kent-Essex	10.9
2. Lambton-Sarnia	3.2
3. Central Erie	5.6
4. Mid-Western	5.9
5. Niagara-Iroquola	18.6
6. Metropolitan	14.0
7. Huronia-Lake Simcoe	4.2
8. Kawartha Lakes	3.1
9. Great Pine Ridge	1.2
10. Bay of Quinte	1.3
11. Hastings-Land O'Lakes	0.4
12. Rideau Lakes-1000 Islands	3.4
13. Seaway Valley	3.8
14. Lower Ottawa Valley	4.7
15. Upper Ottawa Valley	1.1
16. Madawaska Valley	0.4
17. Haliburton	0.7
18. Muskoka	2.2
19. Grey-Bruce	2.8
20. Parry Sound-Georgian Bay	0.8
21. Algonquin Park	0.5

Figure 17-10(b). Tourist visitors to Southern Ontario—tourist or vacation areas as a percentage of total visitors to the province, 1968.

17-9. Decide on a graded-shading scheme[14] to show the following groups of visitors:
　less than 1%
　1 to 5.9%
　6 to 10%
　Over 10%

Using the data from Figure 17-10(b) colour in a tracing of Figure 17-10(a) according to this graded-shading scheme and compare it with the maps of assignments 17-6 and 17-7. Write down the ways the maps differ and offer an explanation.

Well, that concludes our land use survey. There wasn't really so much to tell you, as you found out a lot for yourself by drawing the maps. Perhaps you now have a better understanding of the way Southern Ontario is structured for play and work. Have you?

18 Trade

John Larke did a good job. In just 15 years between 1896 and 1911 he saw Canada's exports to Australia rise from $518 233 to $3 900 000, an increase of over 750%.

John Larke was Canada's first full-time Trade Commissioner. Before 1895, when he was appointed, there had been a number of people interested in fostering Canada's growing trade, but they were all part-timers, and they all had other work to do as well. John Larke represented Canada's developing interest in its world-wide trade. Since that time, Canada has opened many Trade Commission offices around the world. Indeed, there are now some 80 offices, staffed by 246 Trade Commissioners, in 57 different countries. The Trade Commissioner Service now forms a $10 million sales organization stretching into every corner of the world, ready at all times to help Canadian businessmen.

Canadian businessmen can also help themselves, of course, and it is only partly a result of the activities of the Trade Commissioners that Canada stands sixth in the world in the value of its foreign trade. There are, in fact, many reasons for Canada's high ranking in trade. Before we go any farther, how many can *you* think of?

Well, how many *did* you think of? Don't say you just skipped on through to here!

One reason, of course, is that Canada has such vast wealth in the form of forests, farms, mines, and so on, and can readily supply the rest of the world with some of the things it wants. Another reason is that Canada cannot produce everything it needs for itself, no bananas or coffee, for example. Still another reason is that Canada makes some things which the rest of the world wants to buy because they think Canada makes them better: midget submarines like the *Pisces,* for instance, and also the computer-controlled electronic price display board for the Tokyo Stock Exchange. Yet another reason is that many Canadians prefer to have a wide choice of things that they think of buying; for example, many Canadians like to have a choice of imported cars, even though they are no better than Canadian-made ones.

all figures in $ million

		exports	imports	total	(s.r.)
1.	U.S.A.	42 590	39 756	82 346	286
2.	West Germany	34 189	29 184	63 373	251
3.	U.K.	19 351	21 724	41 075	202
4.	Japan	19 318	18 881	38 199	199
5.	France	17 742	18 780	36 522	191
6.	Canada	16 187	13 360	29 547	172
7.	Italy	13 210	14 939	28 149	167
8.	Netherlands	11 766	13 393	25 159	158
9.	U.S.S.R.	12 800	11 739	24 539	156
10.	Belgium	11 609	11 362	22 971	151

Figure 18-1.   The world's top ten countries by value of international trade, 1970.

18-1.   Figure 18-1 lists the top ten countries by value of international trade. Using this information, construct located proportional circles[4] on a world map to show the distribution of the main trading countries. Divide[5] the circles according to the percentage of total value created by exports.

You will notice from your answer that most of the trading nations appear to be in Europe. This is partly because there are so many countries *in* Europe that it is very easy for products to cross international frontiers and so get counted as international trade. Imagine the very high figures you could get for Ontario if you had to count all the interprovincial trade as well as the international trade! Still, there's nothing we can do about all the countries in Europe; we'll just have to take the figures as they are, remembering all the time that, despite the "inflated" figures for the European countries, Canada still ranks sixth.

If you want to get a fuller picture of Canada's place in the world in the matter of foreign trade, then you must look at two more sets of figures as well (Figures 18-2 and 18-3).

		1970 total trade $ million	1970 population millions
1.	U.S.A.	82 346	204.8
2.	West Germany	63 373	59.4
3.	U.K.	41 075	55.7
4.	Japan	38 199	103.4
5.	France	36 522	50.8
6.	Canada	29 547	21.4
7.	Italy	28 149	53.7
8.	Netherlands	25 159	13.0
9.	U.S.S.R.	24 539	242.8
10.	Belgium	22 971	9.7

Figure 18-2.   Total trade value and population for ten countries.

		1970 GDP $ million	1970 exports $ million
1.	U.S.A.	969 574	42 590
2.	West Germany	186 743	34 189
3.	U.K.	118 535	19 351
4.	Japan	197 623	19 318
5.	France	147 311	17 742
6.	Canada	78 704	16 187
7.	Italy	92 699	13 210
8.	Netherlands	30 638	11 766
9.	U.S.S.R.	325 000*	12 800
10.	Belgium	25 488	11 609

*Net Material Product.

Figure 18-3.   GDP and export values for ten countries.

18-2.   Calculate the value of total foreign trade per person for each of the ten countries listed, and then place a ranking number (from 1 to 10) against each country. For example, Canada's value of foreign trade per person is $1380.70, and it ranks third. Draw an ordered horizontal bar graph[1] to illustrate the results, colouring Canada in red and all the other countries in a quite different colour, like pale blue.

18-3.   Using the data in Figure 18-3, calculate the value of exports as a percentage of the Gross Domestic Product (GDP); then allocate a ranking number from 1 to 10, and construct a bar graph[1] to illustrate the results. What do you think the figure GDP represents? Well, almost! It's quite like GNP in a way, but it measures just the value of all the things that a country produces *domestically,* and it doesn't count all the things that a country might bring in from abroad. Can you now see why we calculate just the *exports* as a percentage of the GDP, and not exports and imports together?

You have now obtained three measures of Canada's place in world trade: first, you have the total values, where it ranks sixth; second, you have the value per person, where it ranks third; and third, you have the value of exports as a percentage of GDP, where it again ranks third. These three measures all tell you different things about Canada's position in world trade. The first measure simply tells you the size of Canada's contribution to world trade, and you can see that it is only about one-third as large as America's contribution and less than half as big as Germany's. But, even so, Canada's contribution is still the sixth largest in the world. The second measure tells you how important foreign trade is — on average — to the people of Canada compared with the people of some other countries. You can see that trade is more important to the people of Belgium and the Netherlands than it is to Canadians, but Canadians rank next, above any other countries. Indeed, you can see that trade is more than three times as important to Canadians as it is to Americans and that it is nearly four times as important as it is to Japanese. The third measure tells you what proportion of each country's domestically produced wealth comes from its earnings in the export trade. Again, only Belgium and the Netherlands rank higher than Canada. You can also see very clearly that Canada depends on its exports for more than twice as much as

Japan depends on *its* exports, and nearly five times as much as the Americans depend upon *their* exports.

Yet another way of looking at Canada's role in world trade is to see where it sells its exports and where it buys its imports. There isn't a country in the world that does not trade in some way or other with Canada, but some of the countries only trade in a very small way. For example, Angola, Paraguay, Gambia, Mauritania, and Burma don't do very much business with Canada, but they do some; indeed, Canada has trading links with all parts of the world.

all figures in $ millions

1970 exports destinations			1970 imports sources	
1.	U.S.A.	10 000	1. U.S.A.	9 900
2.	U.K.	1 400	2. U.K.	740
3.	Japan	730	3. Japan	580
4.	West Germany	350	4. West Germany	370
5.	Netherlands	260	5. Venezuela	340
6.	Australia	190	6. France	160
7.	Belgium	180	7. Australia	150
8.	Italy	170	8. Italy	145

Figure 18-4. Exports and imports, chief countries.

18-4. Obtain two maps of the world. On one, draw arrows pointing out from Canada to the main export customers as shown in Figure 18-4. Make the width of the arrows proportional to the value of the exports to each country.[11] On the second map, draw proportional-width arrows[11] pointing from the various sources of imports into Canada. Shade the arrows in the two maps so that exports look different from imports. And don't forget the titles.

When it comes to the matter of carrying exports and imports around the world, Canada doesn't do so well. Even though Canada generates the sixth largest value of trade in the world, it ranks way down when it comes to providing shipping services. In merchant shipping (Figure 18-5) it ranks sixteenth, and in air-freight, where it does better, it ranks eighth (Figure 18-6).

1970
cubic metres capacity
(2.83 cubic metres = 1 GRT)

1.	Liberia	109 102 160
2.	Japan	86 340 470
3.	U.K.	77 358 050
4.	Norway	61 467 600
5.	U.S.A.	46 032 780
6.	U.S.S.R.	45 829 020
7.	Greece	36 976 780
8.	West Germany	24 561 570
9.	Italy	23 033 370
10.	France	19 841 130
.		
.		
.		
16.	Canada	6 695 780

Figure 18-5. The world's largest national merchant shipping fleets.

		1970 tonne-kilometres
1.	U.S.A.	1 749 632 000
2.	U.K.	502 236 000
3.	West Germany	476 867 000
4.	France	457 307 000
5.	Netherlands	382 756 000
6.	Japan	328 268 000
7.	Italy	272 019 000
8.	Canada	210 394 000
9.	Belgium	186 500 000
10.	Switzerland	172 927 000

Figure 18-6.   Air freight, chief countries.

18-5.   Write down all the reasons you can think of for Canada's low ranking in the provision of merchant shipping services. Maybe if you're stuck on this you can have a class discussion about it; or perhaps your teacher will help you.

Before we leave the study of trade, we should answer your question. For the last little while you have undoubtedly been eager to ask about the part played by invisible trade. Well, we cannot answer all the points about it here and now, but we can give you an indication of the answer. You know, of course, that invisible trade deals with things like tourist earnings, insurance and banking earnings, and other transfers of money from one country to another in return for services rendered. Clearly, your answer to question 18-5 will tell you some of the reasons for Canada's poor performance in providing shipping services. Perhaps to bring everything back to a happier level, we should just take a look at tourist earnings (Figure 18-7). These show that Canada ranks sixth in the world, which is where we came in!

		$ millions
1.	U.S.A.	2 319
2.	Spain	1 681
3.	Italy	1 639
4.	Mexico	1 454
5.	France	1 322
6.	Canada	1 185
7.	U.K.	1 039
8.	West Germany	1 024
9.	Austria	999
10.	Switzerland	905

Figure 18-7.   1970 international tourist receipts, chief countries.

19 Occupational Change

MAN THE CHOOSER

"Rupert Weyburn looked at his watch slowly and then on out to the fields. He could not see the detail out in the fields, but he knew that his wheat crop, the one he had laboured over, was ready for harvesting. Behind him lay the shiny, big, brand new, red machine. It promised a lot. Rupert hoped it would deliver. It had to, because Rupert had laid off two of his old helpers; the machine would do their work."

"As Bob pulled the irrigation wheels over to the next location, he thought to himself that it would soon be dark. He had put a lot of hours into the irrigation project today, and he was tired. Perhaps next month he would start to look around for some work that didn't take up his entire day."

"The bus from along the coast came to a stop in the downtown terminal. A few old women got out, come to look at the stores; and also a few young men. The men, mostly in their early twenties, looked round inside the bus depot, knowing neither each other nor anyone else in this strange town. Eventually, a few bought the local newspaper and started to circle some of the jobs they would apply for. At least it beats fishing, thought some of them, while others hoped it would provide more security."

And so people in various places and at various times change their jobs. Some change because they have to; some change because they want to. And in nearly all cases it's an individual decision. Large groups of people together hardly ever decide anything. Indeed, they are more likely to argue about things than to decide things. Decisions, especially over important things like which job you want to work at, are individual matters.

Nevertheless, it often happens that a lot of people make the same sort of decision at about the same time. And they do it, like the young men on the bus, without even knowing each other. People often do the same things together without planning to, without even giving a thought as to what other people might do. How many times, for instance, have you travelled on a bus to somewhere and not known anyone on the bus?

It is in this way that common actions get taken by a lot of separate people. Each makes his or her own decisions, independently of all the others; but they all make the same decision!

One of the most common decisions that people have taken over the last 100 years or so in Canada has been to quit the farms and look for work in the towns.

all data in percent of working population

	1871	1881	1891	1901	1911	1921	1931	1941	1951	1961	1971
rural	80.4	74.3	68.2	65.2	58.3	54.7	50.3	49.1	37.1	28.9	23.9
urban	19.6	25.7	31.8	34.8	41.7	45.3	49.7	50.9	62.9	71.1	76.1

Figure 19-1. The changing rural-urban occupancy pattern in Canada, 1871-1971.

19-1. Construct a simple graph to show the changing distribution of population in Canada, using the data in Figure 19-1. Colour the rural line in green and the urban line in red.

It's easy to think of many reasons why people leave farmwork. We have already come across two or three. They may be replaced by machinery on the farm; they may prefer the shorter and more regular hours in town work; or they may think that town-work offers more security (how?).

19-2. There are several reasons why people leave farms and come instead to work in towns (did you notice that word *come* instead of *go*?). What do you think are some of the reasons in Canada? Ask around.

Automatically, when people come to work in towns they have to find a change in job; they don't want the same sort of work even if it's available, but usually it's not even available. A migration to the towns therefore usually means an occupational change, too. And that means that the whole economy has to change. You can't have urban migration to the extent that it has happened in Canada over the last 100 years without some pretty widely growing alternative in the way of employment. Nor can you have it without the remaining farmers becoming a lot more efficient, because all the extra people in the towns still have to be fed.

To a certain extent the two things go together: there is alternative employment, and the farmers do get to be more efficient. The link is in the creation of town-based jobs like making harvesters and milking machines, or refrigeration units and pesticides, or transportation systems and fertilizers. All of these things help both the new urban workers and the remaining farmers. Such activities are technically called secondary occupations, and they are essential if the people off the farms want to have a choice of jobs. Canada has a very diversified range of secondary (or manufacturing) activity, and so its people are a lot luckier than those of some other countries. The very wide choice of secondary jobs in Canada is partly a result of local businessmen seizing the opportunities of available labour from the farms to set up their own business: just like Massey and Harris and Ferguson setting up a farm equipment factory (which is now part of one of the biggest farm equipment companies in the world — Massey-Ferguson Ltd.). The very wide choice is also partly a result of American businessmen setting up factories in Canada because the Canadian governments of the day would not allow the Americans to sell a lot of their goods in Canada if the goods were made in America (the Canadian governments of the past therefore encouraged Americans to set up branch plants inside Canada). Canadians have a wide choice of manufacturing jobs, then, partly because of their own actions and partly because of the actions of Americans.

One of the characteristics of the North American economies is the almost constant inventions which occur. New and better machines are designed, and more goods can be made even more efficiently than previously. Over a period of time, this constant improvement in machinery has caused factories to employ relatively fewer people to make relatively more goods. And thus a second source of job-seeking labour is created (the first, you remember, was the increasingly efficient farms). As the factories become more efficient, less factory labour is needed, and people start to look for other work.

What other work is there?

Right. There's all the work in stores, in repair and maintenance, in transportation, in offices of various types, in banks, in communication, in entertainment, in public utilities (what are *they*?), in education, in health, in the tourist business, and so on. All these jobs have one thing in common: they provide services of one sort or another for people directly. These are collectively called tertiary activities, and they are now the most rapidly growing sector of the economy as far as jobs are concerned.

all data in percent of working population

occupation class	1881	1901	1921	1941	1951	1961	1971
primary*	51.2	44.3	36.6	29.3	20.7	16.8	8.4
secondary**	29.4	27.8	26.5	26.3	32.6	31.7	26.8
tertiary***	19.4	27.9	36.9	44.4	46.9	51.3	64.8

*primary includes farming, forestry, fishing, and mining
**secondary includes construction and manufacturing
***tertiary includes all services

Figure 19-2. The changing occupational structure of the Canadian labour force, 1881-1971.

19-3. Using the data in Figure 19-2, draw a multiple-line graph[8] to show the changing occupational structure of the Canadian population. Make the three lines quite distinct from each other in colour, and label the lines directly (do NOT use a legend).

As the range of tertiary jobs expands, the people of Canada have an increasingly wide choice of work. Almost anything you want to do, you can do (if you're prepared to work for it). Some people would even say that in Canada today there is a choice of whether to work or not. That's something that never existed before. At one time not so long ago, you worked or you starved. Nowadays, there is a choice — work or welfare. And within the work choice there is a vast variety of things you could do.

So how do you make a choice?

Obviously, there are many things that influence your decision as to what sort of work you do. One of the least important now is feeling that you should do the same sort of work your father did; you tend to make up your mind from other evidence. You look at job openings (and you know what category is now the most popular, don't you?); you look at the studying you might need to do; you look at the interests that you have; and you look at the sort of rewards you might expect from a job (wages, time off, "perks," and so on).

Every yead the Department of National Revenue in Ottawa publishes a survey of incomes, broken down by job and by region. Doctors, for instance, tend to earn the highest wages in Canada as a group; but they don't earn the same everywhere. Strangely, they earn above average wages in poor Newfoundland, while they earn way-below average wages in rich British Columbia. Farmers, as a group, tend to earn the smallest incomes across the country (60% of registered farmers didn't even earn enough in 1972 to pay any income tax at all!); but they are worst off in the poor Maritimes, while rich British Columbia rewards them in a well-above average fashion. As you should by now expect, the highest incomes are concentrated in the cities. Half of all Canadian taxpayers live in the largest 100 cities, but they pay nearly 75% of all income taxes. The career opportunities in the smaller towns and in rural areas are clearly limited if you rate rewards highly when you are choosing a job. Among the cities, you can probably guess where the ones right at the top are located. In Ontario and British Columbia, which are the chief destinations of immigrants and people from the other provinces, of course.

Forestry	84.2	Highway construction	81.0
Gold mining	45.4	Air services	161.2
Iron mining	135.1	Railway services	84.2
Petroleum mining	144.0	Truck transport	135.0
Tobacco processing	95.4	Highway maintenance	113.0
Shoe making	86.0	Post office	141.3
Cotton textiles	78.2	Electricity generation	124.6
Synthetic textiles	126.4	Retail trade	142.8
Furniture making	129.7	Food stores	151.6
Iron and steel mills	137.6	Financial institutions	148.2
Hardware and tools	163.0	Recreational services	161.3
Machinery making	153.2	Business services	194.8
Car making	166.6	Miscellaneous services	223.5
Communications equipment	171.7	Total employment average	127.1
Shipbuilding	92.5		
Petroleum refineries	93.8		
Chemicals	120.5		

Figure 19-3.   Index numbers for employment in selected occupations, *Canada Year-book, 1972.*

19-4.   Figure 19-3 contains a selection of index numbers for a variety of jobs across Canada. The index base is 1961, so you can easily see which jobs have gained by expansion and which have suffered through contraction since that time. Construct an ordered positive-negative bar graph[20] of the index numbers and then write down any conclusions you may have about the figures.

Corner Brook	125.77	Guelph	120.93
St. John's	100.20	Hamilton	135.49
Halifax	105.77	Kingston	121.24
Sydney	111.62	Kitchener	116.13
Moncton	98.79	London	121.41
St. John	105.50	Niagara Falls	120.45
Chicoutimi	143.12	North Bay	126.84
Drummondville	100.52	Oshawa	145.56
Granby	101.64	Ottawa	120.00
Montreal	125.45	Peterborough	131.17
Quebec	109.84	St. Catharines	139.88
Rouyn-Noranda	124.91	St. Thomas	141.15
St. Hyacinthe	96.25	Sarnia	161.99
St. Jerome	103.61	Sault Ste. Marie	149.19
Shawinigan	126.79	Stratford	110.95
Sherbrooke	107.49	Sudbury	159.21
Sorel	143.91	Thunder Bay	124.69
Thetford Mines	130.63	Timmins	116.59
Trois Rivières	117.25	Toronto	133.67
Valleyfield	129.81	Welland	149.01
Belleville	110.54	Windsor	150.80
Brampton	128.93	Woodstock	117.65
Brantford	117.18	Winnipeg	108.84
Brockville	124.19	Regina	110.64
Chatham	129.12	Saskatoon	109.12
Cornwall	119.80	Calgary	126.73
		Edmonton	121.80
		Vancouver	133.90
		Victoria	117.30

Figure 19-4.   Average weekly wages and salaries in dollars for selected urban areas, *Canada Yearbook, 1972.*

19-5.   Using the data in Figure 19-4, prepare a map of Canada as follows: put a small circle at the location of each urban area mentioned in Figure 19-4, colour-coded to the following scale

under $100 — pale yellow (PALE yellow)

$100 to $119.99 — pale (pale) red

$120 to $139.99 — bright red

$140 and over — bright orange (bright, bright)

Now that you've finished the map, do you think that's all there is to it? How about some conclusions?

20 The Okanagan Valley

REGIONALISM

Slashed into the plateau-lands of the extreme southern portion of the interior of British Columbia are four or five southward-draining valleys. The Okanagan is the westernmost of these valleys; others to the east of it include the Kettle valley, the Granby valley, the Arrow Lakes valley (otherwise called the Columbia valley), and the Kootenay valley. All of these valleys open southwards to the United States, and all were first occupied by people moving up

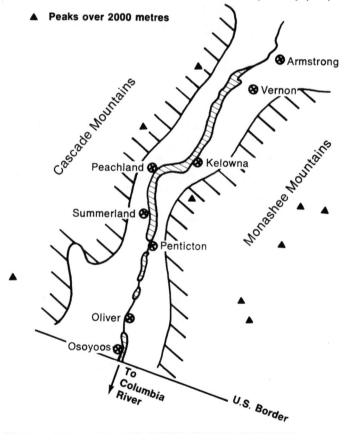

Figure 20-1. The Okanagan valley.

from the States. Communication east and west with other parts of Canada is not naturally easy; north-south ridges of land (the remains of the Fraser plateau) separate these southern British Columbia valleys not only from each other but also from other parts of Canada, while nowadays the frontier of the 49th Parallel has a closing effect on the southern end of the valleys. The valleys therefore tend to be rather isolated. But not unattractive to man. Despite their isolation, they exert a remarkable pull on population. The Okanagan valley (see Figure 20-1) was first exploited by Europeans in the early 1800s, when fur traders set up dealings with local Indians. Gold was subsequently discovered in 1833, but the discoveries were kept a secret until the 1850s for fear of ruining the fur trade. The first European settlement occurred with the founding of a mission in 1859 at what is now called Mission Creek, just south of Kelowna. And shortly after, as the gold mining fever moved farther north, there followed a wave of cattle ranchers moving in from Oregon and Washington (why?). Forest exploitation soon developed in parts of the valley, but the major development was the growing of fruit.

The first fruit trees (apple) were planted by the mission fathers in 1862; other trees were planted by the ranchers who moved in during the remainder of the 1860s; and then in 1892 commercial apple production was shown to be feasible by the success of large plantings near Vernon and Kelowna by Lord Aberdeen. The next 20-30 years saw considerable progress in the development of settlements geared to fruit production; and the Okanagan valley thus became famous as one of the chief fruit growing districts in Canada (and the world).

Why is the valley so suitable to fruit growing? Well, the chief reasons are climatic, because you certainly can't say that the valley has any advantages with regard to easy access to market. So let's take a closer look at the climate.

Most people regard British Columbia as a very wet province and a very mild one. In general terms this is true, but in detail you will find that there are lots of exceptions. The Okanagan valley is one of the exceptions. For a start it is almost desert. And then it is also quite extreme as well. It also gets much more sunshine than the average place in British Columbia (Figure 20-2). And it tends to accumulate more heat in summer.

20-1. Using the precipitation and temperature data from Figure 20-2, construct hythergraphs[19] for each of the five places mentioned. Use five different colours for clarity. Write down your conclusions about the differences in basic climate between the five places.

20-2. This time use the information from Figure 20-2 regarding hours of bright sunshine and quantity of degree-days above 6°C. Set up a graph with hours of sunshine up the vertical or y axis (scaled from 0 to 350), and quantity of degree-days along the horizontal or x axis (scaled from 0 to whatever you need to accommodate the highest single monthly figure for any one of the five places). Construct a graph similar to a hythergraph, but plotting in the monthly co-ordinates for sunshine and degree-days instead of for temperature and precipitation. When you have finished — in five different colours, of course — you should be able to see just how different the Okanagan valley is from other parts of British Columbia. Write down your conclusions.

	Penticton				Prince George				Prince Rupert				Vancouver				Victoria			
	1	2	3	4	1	2	3	4	1	2	3	4	1	2	3	4	1	2	3	4
J	2.5	−3	52	0	4.7	−10	57	0	24.0	2	40	0	20.1	3	48	0	10.3	4	66	5
F	2.0	0	90	0	3.8	−7	88	0	18.9	3	59	0	15.3	4	80	10	8.0	6	94	30
M	1.9	4	150	10	3.2	0	133	0	20.1	4	81	15	13.3	7	126	90	5.5	7	148	90
A	2.1	10	198	110	2.4	5	175	30	17.3	6	103	60	9.2	10	168	170	3.0	9	197	130
M	2.5	14	238	260	3.9	10	242	150	13.0	9	138	180	6.9	13	226	200	2.5	12	252	220
J	3.5	18	247	375	5.6	14	240	270	10.0	12	125	250	5.4	16	223	300	2.3	14	263	280
J	2.0	21	312	465	5.4	16	254	330	11.9	13	125	330	3.5	18	280	400	1.2	16	322	340
A	2.1	19	279	425	5.7	15	244	300	13.9	14	125	380	4.1	18	254	400	1.7	16	287	340
S	2.3	15	204	285	5.6	10	161	180	20.4	12	97	290	8.0	15	178	280	3.3	14	205	320
O	2.5	9	140	120	5.4	5	100	40	31.3	9	54	220	16.7	11	110	180	7.4	11	130	190
N	2.6	3	59	0	5.4	−2	53	0	31.2	6	40	80	17.5	7	53	60	9.2	7	72	90
D	3.1	0	40	0	5.2	−8	38	0	26.7	3	31	10	24.2	4	38	10	20.0	5	57	15

Legend: 1. average precipitation in centimetres
2. average temperature in °C
3. total hours of bright sunshine
4. degree-days above 6°C (6°C marks the beginning and end of the growing season)

Figure 20-2. Climatic data for selected stations in British Columbia.

Even with its climatic advantages for fruit growing, the Okanagan valley still has some problems. The obvious problem of isolation from large markets has been partly overcome by co-operation among the farmers. Marketing of nearly all the fruit grown is controlled by the British Columbia Fruit Growers Association, which is really a co-operative of all the farmers. By means of inspection, grading, sampling and bulk transportation, the fruit from the Okanagan is successfully marketed as far afield as Ontario. But its main markets are in British Columbia and the Prairies.

Another problem is the extreme winters, which tend every so often to produce frosts which kill off the fruit trees. This means that there is frequent re-planting in the orchards, dead trees being replaced on an "as-it-happens" basis. In spring and fall, the farmers can successfully take some precautions against frost (such as using oil-pots and giant fans), but in winter these are of little use. Prices inevitably have to cover the costs of such activities, and if fruit prices are low, then the fruit growers may be pushed out of production. If they are pushed out of business (and several have been), then they usually find ready buyers for their land among the people who are getting ready to retire from work in places like Vancouver. Such people are only too willing to buy up a piece of land in the sunny countryside; there are now many retired people in the Okanagan.

The normal problems of spring and fall frosts in fruit orchards are met by the normal solutions: by not planting on the flat bottom-lands unless you have no choice, in other words. Normally, cold air on a hillside drains down into the floor of the valley; if the cold air is below freezing point, then you get what are called frost-hollows being formed on the valley floor. The best place to plant fruit trees that are sensitive to frosts is therefore not on the valley floor but on the valley side, where the frosty air drains straight past. The fruit trees of the Okanagan are easily grown on the valley sides. And in any event the floor of the valley is mostly occupied by lakes.

The valley sides are not all suitable for fruit trees, of course. In some places the land is too steep, and in others the soil is too poor. The best parts are the silty terraces, especially those which face south or west to get maximum sunshine. The silty terraces themselves are the product of deposition in lakes ponded by glaciers in the Ice Age at levels higher than the present lakes. The old glaciers have long since disappeared, but the silty terraces remain.

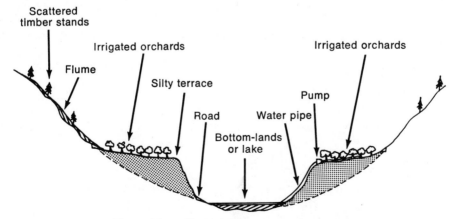

Figure 20-3. Typical Okanagan cross-section.

Even the silty terraces are not ideal, because they are short of water. Precipitation is slight, as you already know; but the obvious alternative water supplies — the lakes — are not easy to use because of the height of the terraces above the lake levels. Pumping is necessary, but then it forms an extra cost. In order to avoid the costs of pumping, some farmers have constructed flumes (*flumes*?) to channel water down from small lakes and streams in the surrounding hills. By these methods, water supplies are assured, and the fruit trees thrive.

Fruit orchards are scattered along the sides of the valley from Vernon down to Osoyoos. There are about 3500 orchards covering about 15 000 hectares and varying considerably in size from the half-hectare hobby plot to the 100-hectare commercial operation. The chief fruit grown is apples (mainly McIntosh, Spartan, and Delicious), followed by pears, peaches, cherries, apricots, and prune-plums. Grapes are also grown on about 1000 hectares and are sold exclusively to local wineries (such as those at Kelowna).

20-3. Construct an ordered horizontal bar graph[1] to illustrate the following data:

	number of trees in the Okanagan valley
apples	1 231 000
pears	380 000
peaches	323 000
cherries	151 000
apricots	143 000
prune-plums	110 000

20-4. Did you find out what degree-days above 6°C means? If not, then you should do so immediately, and not be so shy of asking about something you don't know next time!

21 Population Trends

CONSTANT CHANGE

When the glaciers melted back and exposed the land surface of Canada, people were already living in North America. In our present state of knowledge we simply do not know whether mankind evolved here but it is well established that people did migrate here, tens of thousands of years ago. They crossed the Bering Strait by boat perhaps, or they could even have walked across without getting wet feet when the sea level was perhaps 100 metres lower than at present. (How could that be?)

The earliest inhabitants of Canada were the Indians and the Eskimos. It is estimated that when John Cabot cruised off Newfoundland the whole North American continent contained fewer than one million people. Of this number, perhaps 250 000 lived in Canada.

A quarter of a million people may seem a small population by present day standards but you must remember that these earliest peoples lived by hunting animals and fish and by gathering roots and berries. Only a few tribes grew crops and no one was entirely dependent on the products of agriculture.

Split by tribal and clan divisions, the native Canadians were not a match technologically for the new waves of settlers. At Confederation in 1867 there were perhaps 3 500 000 Canadians. In the next hundred years that figure was to expand by more than five times.

It is obviously important that a country know fairly exactly how many people it has. How many reasons can you think of for this? When a country determines to find out how many people it contains, it holds a census. Canada holds a full census every ten years (1961, 1971, etc.) with smaller samplings of the population five years after every census (1956, 1966, etc.).

1871	3.7	1931	10.4
1881	4.3	1941	11.5
1891	4.8	1951	14.0
1901	5.4	1961	18.2
1911	7.2	1966	20.0
1921	8.8	1971	21.6

Figure 21-1.   The growth of Canada's population. All figures in millions.

21-1.   Construct a time-series line graph to show the figures in Figure 21-1. Don't slip up over the time scale!

Has the growth of Canada's population been regular or not? Look carefully at the years from 1901 to 1941, and from 1950 to 1971.

Now why on earth would a population grow erratically? Let's think for a moment. People are born, live for an unforeseeable length of time, and then die. It is quite likely that changes in the numbers of people being born and the rate at which they die will cause a change in the rate of growth of the population. Does that seem reasonable to you? At any event, examine Figure 21-2.

	Birth rate	Death rate
1921	29.3	11.6
1926	24.7	11.4
1931	23.2	10.2
1936	20.3	9.9
1941	22.4	10.1
1946	27.2	9.4
1951	27.2	9.0
1956	28.0	8.2
1961	26.1	7.7
1966	19.4	7.5
1971	17.4	7.3

Figure 21-2. Canadian vital statistics: all rates are in persons per thousand total population.

21-2. Construct a multiple-line time-series graph[8] to show the data in Figure 21-2. Shade the space between the line for births and the line for deaths and call it "Canada's Natural Increase." Why is that title used? How could a population grow "unnaturally"? (There is only one way!)

Somewhere on the graph you have drawn is the "bulge." Use your own method to show it.

The "bulge" was a post-war increase in the rate at which babies were born. Returning soldiers married if they hadn't done so before going overseas. Peace and rising expectations reversed the trend of a falling birth rate during the hungry 'thirties. Now, if you compare the graph from assignment 21-1 and the graph from assignment 21-2, you should be able to spot something that looks a little hard to explain. No? Just read on!

21-3. Why did Canada's population continue to grow during the 1930s although during that time period the rate at which babies were being born declined?

Today, the postwar "bulge" or "baby boom" has ended. New birth control devices and organisations such as Zero Population Growth (ZPG) have contributed to the declining birth rate. So has prosperity — can you suggest why?

It is worthwhile mentioning that the "bulge" gave rise to effects on the Canadian economy and social scene which are still working themselves out in the 1970s.

21-4. Canada's school leaving age is 16 years. High school graduates are aged between 18 and 20 years on average. University graduates of all types have ages anywhere between 21 and 28. Can you suggest some ways in which the "bulge" years still affect the Canadian economy and Canadian society?

Throughout most of the period from 1921 to the present day, the death rate has declined pretty steadily. Medical research and new treatments such as insulin for diabetes (discovered by Banting, a Canadian) have allowed people to live longer. It is nowadays a far cry from the mid-nineteenth century when a pioneer farmer had a large family for a workforce and as a form of old-age insurance. People died young in those days. At Confederation a newborn baby could expect to live less than 50 years on average. Virulent diseases like cholera, typhoid, diphtheria, and tuberculosis carried off many people. Babies had only an even chance of surviving their first year and at least 20 times as many mothers died then in child-birth as do today. Modern diseases of the heart, Canada's biggest killer today, were then almost unknown. People died of something more deadly, sooner. Today people live longer only to succumb to more slow-acting fatal influences.

Today, some people think that Canada is close to ZPG. If a married couple has only two children they are not even maintaining the population. If we want to offset losses of people due to accidents and compensate for those people who choose to remain childless, then the number of children per family should be 2.1. At the moment in Canada, the average family size is around 2.4.

If ZPG ever comes about, the only way to increase Canada's population will be by immigration.

Well, what has been the result of all these changes in the vital statistics of Canada? How have the people themselves changed?

Age group	1871	1971
0-4	14.6	8.5
5-9	14.0	10.3
10-14	12.8	10.6
15-19	11.4	9.8
20-24	9.4	8.8
25-29	7.6	7.3
30-34	6.0	7.3
35-39	5.1	5.9
40-44	4.3	6.0
45-49	3.8	4.6
50-54	3.1	4.9
55-59	2.4	4.4
60-64	1.9	3.5
65-69	1.5	2.8
70 +	2.1	5.3
	100.0%	100.0%

Figure 21-3. The age structure of Canada's population for two selected census years. Both sexes are included.

Clearly, Canada's population increase is due in some part to an increased expectancy of life. We have noted this earlier. Did you know that there are almost as many Canadians over 65 years of age today as there were Canadians in the entire population of Canada at Confederation?

	Male	Female
1931	60	62
1941	63	66
1951	66	71
1956	68	73
1961	68	74
1966	69	75
1971	69	76

Figure 21-4. Life expectancy table (years) at birth in Canada.

The places of residence of Canadians have also changed over the years. The early settlers were farmers who cleared the land they were granted or had bought cheaply. The pioneer and his family cleared their own land and grew crops on many-hectared farms. Transportation was poor and the road system only suitable for travel during summer and fall. Farming families often saw no strangers for weeks or months at a time. Most of Canada's people were rural people living in a rhythm decreed by the seasons. Gradually though, wealth wrung from the land was accumulated and put by. Store clothes were worn, rather than homespun. Children were sent to school, and roads were paved or given more maintenance. Governments extended in scope, and the industrial revolution offered goods for sale to everyone who had the money to buy them. Towns grew to become cities and the urban population worked in factories or provided services.

These early towns and cities and villages acted like people—magnets. People left marginal farms or poor fishing villages and looked for a better life in places like Quebec, Toronto, Halifax, and Montreal. The trend of an increasing urban population is one which affects the whole world today. Towns become more densely populated and the people left to work the land become fewer in number. They can keep food production high, though, only by using machinery, fertilizer, and better seed, all of which are produced by the towns. It is clear then that the farmer couldn't survive without the townsman to provide much of his equipment. Equally, the townsman relies on the food sent to his urban area by the farmer.

	Rural	Urban
1891	71	29
1901	65	35
1911	58	42
1921	50	50
1931	46	54
1941	37	63
1951	33	67
1961	30	70
1966	26	74
1971	24	76

Figure 21-5. Rural-urban components of Canada's population. Figures in percent.

21-7. Construct a compound line graph[9] to show the data in Figure 21-5. Do you think Canada's population will ever become completely urban or not?

In this short study, we have been able only to scratch the surface of some of the trends that have influenced Canadians for at least the past century. Are you aware of a population trend from the tables that we haven't covered here and can you guess at its possible influence on us all? Go on, think about it as quickly as you can. We are none of us getting any younger!

22 Single-industry Towns

SUPPORT OF LIFE

Not many towns actually have their main street paved with gold. Kirkland Lake has. It's not solid gold, of course, otherwise by now someone would probably have tried to run off with the main street. It's actually gold ore, and it's not on the top paving but underneath it as the roadbed. And it was all a mistake, anyway, because the company that was paving the road took the ballast rock from the gold ore store rather than from the waste rock pile in error, and by the time the mistake was realized the gold ore had been paved over. Since there was more gold ore in the ground they decided not to pull the road up.

In fact, over a billion dollars' worth of gold was mined in Kirkland Lake, creating millionaires and disappointed men in the process. One of the most noteworthy of the millionaires was Harry Oakes, who started his claims in 1911. One of the stories about Harry Oakes is that he was so poor when he started that he had to be aided by Hymie and Max Kaplan, who ran the general store, and by Charlie Chow, who ran the restaurant. When he started to become rich, Oakes offered these people a choice: either take the cash for all the debts or take shares in the Lake Shore Mine, the shares selling at that time for a few cents each. The Kaplans took the cash, and regretted it later. Charlie Chow took the shares, and he didn't regret it. The Lake Shore Mine pulled over a quarter of a billion dollars' worth of gold out of the ground before it closed in 1968! By that time, however, Harry Oakes was dead: he was murdered in the Bahamas in 1943, and the case is still unsolved.

Single-industry towns are not all gold-mining towns filled with millionaires, however. There are many different types of single-industry town. Some of them are mining towns, but for other minerals besides gold; some of them are pulp and paper towns; some of them are smelting towns; some of them are ports; some are tourist towns; and so on. So let's have a closer look at towns and their functions.

Towns generally provide services. The services are pretty obvious in most cases: there are stores, colleges, hospitals, lots of lawyers and doctors and dentists; there are big-league sports teams in big centres and minor league sports teams in small centres; there are theatres and bookstores; there are agents and arrangers, fixers and organizers; there are hotels and restaurants for travellers; there are radio stations; and there are many other things, services all. For many towns, the provision of services is crucial to their existence, and if people stopped coming in from surrounding areas the towns would really suffer.

Other towns rely on manufacturing. Often, a variety of goods may be produced, and sometimes the list is longer than you could possibly remember. Who can say what Toronto makes? And at other times the list may be quite short, so that the town is virtually a single-industry town (how about Oakville? or Oshawa?). When a town relies on manufacturing, however, it usually also has a large element of commerce, with banks, shipping agents, trust companies, transportation provision, and so on as well.

Single-industry towns are different. They are towns that rely on a single industry. They may have other things happening as well: there may well be restaurants and hotels, a movie theatre, radio station, hospital, and college. But the town doesn't rely on these things. They are just there for the convenience of the inhabitants. The town relies on whatever the single industry is. And if that wasn't there, then the town would die. Just like Dawson City did after the Yukon gold rush ended.

We can broadly pick out three different categories of single-industry towns: those based on resource exploitation, those based on processing, and those based on the provision of very specialized services.

Mines are the chief form of resource exploitation giving rise to towns. Lumbering more usually gives rise to camps, though there are a few lumber towns; Happy Valley in Labrador is an example. Fishing generally supports towns, such as Lunenburg and Yarmouth in Nova Scotia, but such towns don't usually rely on fishing in quite the same way that a mining town relies on the mines. So, while noting lumber towns and fishing towns, let's concentrate on mining towns.

Since the beginnings of exploration in Canada, people have known of the existence of minerals. Jacques Cartier reported gold from the city of "Saganna," but no one was ever able to locate it precisely. It was most likely somewhere in Ontario, except for the descriptions by Cartier of the people of Saganna: "men who fly, having wings on their arms like bats, although they flew but little from the ground to a tree or from the tree to the ground."

The real surge towards the exploitation of minerals in Ontario came in the early 1900s. Sudbury nickel and copper had been worked for a few years, but there was nothing really exciting happening. Farmers were gradually pushing into the Clay Belt of northern Ontario, and the railway was following them. Two tie men employed by the railway noticed metallic particles in a rock-cut one day and sent samples for assay. The report stated a concentration of 125 kilograms per tonne, which was fantastic. It was 1903; the tiemen were called McKinley and Darragh. Cobalt's first mining claim was by the McKinley-Darragh Mine. Another claim was filed by Fred LaRose, who threw his blacksmith's hammer at a fox, missed the fox, broke open a chunk of rock instead, and found it was the tip of a rich silver vein.

It was these discoveries, and the money they created, that led to the later developments. Other prospectors, such as Sandy McIntyre, Benny Hollinger, and Jules and Noah Timmins moved in and found gold. The main finds were made in the Porcupine district, where the Timmins brothers founded a town in 1912. From the Porcupine field, over one and a half billion dollars' worth of gold has been extracted!

22-1. Enlarge the map in Figure 22-1 to full-page size. On it, plot proportional circles[4] over the appropriate mines to illustrate the value of gold extracted (see Figure 22-2).

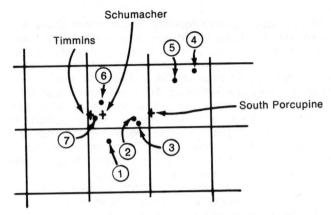

Figure 22-1. The chief gold mines in the Timmins-Porcupine district of northern Ontario.

Mines	Approximate total value of gold output at historic prices in $	(s.r.)
1. Aunor	75 000 000	8660
2. Dome	300 000 000	17320
3. Preston	60 000 000	7746
4. Pamour Porcupine	75 000 000	8660
5. Hallnor	50 000 000	7071
6. McIntyre Porcupine	350 000 000	18710
7. Hollinger	600 000 000	24490

Figure 22-2. Output of the chief gold mines in the Timmins-Porcupine district.

The days of happy (happy? more like ecstatic) chance discovery are now gone. Prospecting is highly organized; big multi-national companies send highly trained men and highly efficient instruments out in teams. But the mining towns are still being created — like Wabush and Labrador City in Newfoundland (1965), Elliot Lake, Ontario (1955), Thompson, Manitoba (1960), and Fort McMurray, Alberta (1967).

Single-industry towns based on processing are usually pulp and paper towns, like Espanola and Marathon in Ontario and Corner Brook in New-foundland. Some of these towns are very old, with ancient mills and out-of-date machinery. They can no longer produce efficiently and competitively and are in danger of being closed down. Ocean Falls in British Columbia recently suffered closure of its mill; the people had mostly gone; the town was becoming a ghost town. And then the provincial government bought out the mill and started it up again! Temiscaming in Quebec faced the same risks: in the late 1960s layoffs were becoming numerous, few young people were being hired, the average age of the workforce in the mill was rising and the average age of people in the town was rising (as young people left). In 1972 it was announced that the mill would be closed for good, and since it was the only industry in the town, the town was not happy. So the workers in the town, with help from the Quebec government, bought out the mill and reopened it! Other pulp and paper towns have brand new mills and are hugely efficient. There is an air of prosperity about these towns, and the future is as assured as it can be. Some of the pulp towns of northern Ontario are of this type.

Other single-industry processing towns are mainly connected in some way with mining, either as smelting centres (Trail in British Columbia, Kitimat in British Columbia, Arvida in Quebec, for instance) or as ports (such as Sept Iles in Quebec). There may also be specialized fish, fruit, and vegetable canning towns, or packing and handling centres, such as Bradford on the Holland Marsh or Leamington in south-western Ontario.

And then finally there is the third sort of single-industry town: the specialized service centre. These are very varied, including towns which provide such services as the provision of power (i.e., Churchill Falls in Labrador), the care of tourists (i.e., Niagara Falls, Ontario), the housing of museum exhibits (e.g., Morrisburg, Ontario), the care of canal traffic (e.g., Welland, Ontario), the trans-shipment of essential cargo (e.g., Hay River, North West Territories), the ferrying of people and goods between the mainland and an island (e.g., Tsawwassen in British Columbia, Port-aux-Basques in Newfoundland), the re-fuelling of aircraft (e.g., Gander in Newfoundland), and the administration of the country (Ottawa in Ontario).

Your teacher will elaborate on most of these for you, if you need it, but let's take a closer look ourselves at two of them: Gander and Ottawa. You all probably know that Gander was built as a re-fuelling stop for the transatlantic airliners that could not make it all the way non-stop from places like Toronto and New York to European cities. But that was before jet aircraft became popular. When jets came into service in the 1950s they could make it all the way non-stop, so Gander faced a real problem: a brand new terminal and no passengers, a town and no jobs. But the first jets were not the last. New jets were being invented and built, chiefly the long-range 747s and DC-10s; so the people at Gander, along with the Ministry of Transport at Ottawa, started a scheme called TOPS — TransOceanic Plane Stop. Can you see how it would work? The idea was to catch the re-fuelling traffic that originated not in Toronto and New York but in Vancouver and San Francisco and other distant places that required a re-fuelling stop on the way to and from Europe. The idea was a great success, and nowadays Gander International has about 40 airlines contracted to use its services. These include such major carriers as Air Canada, Eastern, Pan Am, TWA, American, El Al, Air France, Lufthansa, KLM, Qantas, LOT Polish Airlines, and the Russian Aeroflot (on its Moscow-Cuba flights).

Ottawa is, of course, unique: it is the national capital. But that's about all it is. It is a single-industry town just like the others we have mentioned. Administration is the only industry in Ottawa worth noting; all the other jobs are there merely to keep the people of Ottawa content and cared for.

22-2. Using the data in Figure 22-3, calculate the degree of specialization for the different centres listed. Do it by drawing up a table similar in appearance to Figure 22-3, and then dividing each figure for each occupational category in each centre by the Canadian average for that occupational category. For example, the figure for Fernie for the managerial category is 11.01% The Canadian average for the managerial category is 8.95%. Divide 11.01 by 8.95, and the answer is 1.23; write this answer down in *your* table under Fernie and opposite managerial. Do the same sort of thing for all the figures for all the centres. You should now be able to see clearly just how specialized some of these towns are. Do you think you can write a paragraph about your conclusions?

Occupational category	Canada average	Dryden Ont.	Timmins Ont.	Fernie B.C.	Kimberley B.C.	Arvida Que.	Asbestos Que.
Managerial	8.95	8.71	6.61	11.01	5.62	5.26	6.89
Professional & Technical	9.72	10.67	8.24	8.63	11.71	23.26	11.00
Clerical	12.89	11.74	9.08	9.76	9.33	12.24	7.67
Sales	6.20	6.13	6.24	5.45	5.71	4.60	5.21
Service & Recreation	12.30	10.80	10.18	12.15	9.90	9.93	8.61
Transport & Communications	6.07	5.51	4.88	7.83	2.48	3.75	6.38
Farming & Fishing	10.59	0.27	0.30	0.23	0.52	0.36	0.36
Logging	1.22	6.31	2.02	2.61	0.67	0.32	0.26
Mining	1.00	—	26.00	13.96	20.43	0.22	15.08
Processing & Production	24.10	29.69	19.00	17.59	27.29	33.33	31.00
General labour	4.86	7.73	3.86	7.49	4.10	4.96	5.18
Others	2.10	2.44	3.59	3.29	2.24	1.77	2.36

Figure 22-3. Occupational statistics, 1961, in percentages of the labour force.

One last word of warning: don't confuse single-industry towns with company towns. All company towns are single-industry towns, but not all single-industry towns are company towns (all blackbirds are birds, but . . .). Company towns are special forms of single-industry towns, because the company virtually owns the entire town. It is most likely to own all the houses (which the workers must leave when they retire), as well as the town newspaper, radio station, perhaps also the hospital, and maybe even the roads (and not just the roads inside the town, but possibly also the only road in and out of the town). Some companies even require their employees to seek permission to buy a car to drive on the company's roads! Probably one of the worst examples of this type of company ownership is Buchans in Newfoundland, where Asarco runs a rich copper-lead-zinc mine. There is naturally a lot of labour trouble in a place like this. Fortunately, not all company towns are of this type: most are well-run and fair to the workers, and indeed in many of these better company towns the employees get better-than-normal benefits, as at Thompson, Manitoba, where the average pay-cheque is way above the Canadian average (indeed, most workers earn over $10 000 a year).

22-3. Plot the figures in Figure 22-4 on a time-series graph,[8] showing clearly how Sudbury earnings are much higher than the Canadian average. Why do you think this is so?

Year:	1961	1962	1963	1964	1965	1966	1967	1968	1969	1970	1971	1972	1973
Canada:	79	80	83	86	91	96	105	111	117	125	130	135	140
Sudbury:	93	95	97	99	101	107	122	130	138	145	153	158	165

Figure 22-4. Average weekly earnings in Canada and Sudbury, in dollars.

23 Trees

RESOURCES

The forests of Canada constitute an important economic resource. They provide employment for a total of some tens of thousands of people, either directly (felling the trees and transporting them) or indirectly (producing paper, plywood and sawn lumber, selling it, etc.).

As you are no doubt aware, a resource is not a resource unless it is utilized. If it is just allowed to stay in the ground or on the ground, it is not being used. It is therefore not a resource in the strictest sense of the term, although some people argue, with a degree of validity, that a forest in an unused state is an aesthetic and recreational resource. In this study it is the commercial value of the forests which we shall deal with.

If you look at an atlas map of the natural vegetation of Canada, you will see that there are several types of forest. Go on, open your atlas!

The *boreal forest* belt occupies 82.1 percent of the forested area of Canada. It consists mainly of conifers, i.e., trees which do not shed their leaves in winter since the leaves (needles) have a small surface area and a thick, waxy outer layer to reduce the loss of water through transpiration in the winter months when they are dormant, or nearly so.

The *subalpine forest* of Alberta and British Columbia takes up 3.7 percent of the forested area of Canada. It is chiefly a coniferous forest.

The *montane forest* occupies the high interior plains of British Columbia and the Kootenay valley. Again, it is mainly coniferous, occupying 2.3 percent of the total area.

The *coastal forest* of British Columbia contains some of the world's tallest trees. It is mainly coniferous and occupies 2.2 percent of the total area.

Over to the east coast now to the *Acadian forest.* This is about evenly mixed of coniferous and deciduous trees. What is a deciduous tree? Two percent of the total forested area is made up of this forest type.

The *Columbia forest* region is found chiefly on the east-facing slopes of the Rockies but at a lower altitude than the subalpine forest. It too is mainly coniferous and occupies 0.8 percent of the area of forested land in Canada.

The *mixed forest* of the Great Lakes-St. Lawrence Lowlands occupies 6.5 percent. To the south, in the mild Lakes peninsula, the *deciduous forest* trees become dominant and while they have mostly been cut down to expose good agricultural land, they occupy 0.4 percent of Canada's forested land.

23-1. Approximately 44.4 percent of Canada's total land area is forested. Show that proportion by means of a divided circle[5] and beside it on the same sheet of paper, construct a percentage bar graph[3] to show the various forest types. Shade coniferous or mainly coniferous forests in green, and mixed forest in brown and green diagonal stripes. Shade the deciduous forest in brown.

140

As you can see from the first assignment, the greater part of Canada's forest is coniferous (not carnivorous!). In fact, there are 140 tree species in Canada and of these, 31 are coniferous with 20 commercial species. The remaining 109 deciduous species yield only about 20 commercially important species too.

It is obviously very important that Canada know just how many trees it has, what type they are, whether it would repay logging them, how long it would take for regeneration after logging, and so on. Various surveys have been made but the largest and most comprehensive (and probably the most accurate) forest inventory was performed in 1968. The results are given in Figure 23-1.

Province	reserved	Merchantable timberland sq. km suitable for regular harvest	not suitable for regular harvest
Newfoundland (Lab.)	300	54 074	33 196
Newfoundland (Isl.)	736	34 916	—
Prince Edward I.	29	2 499	—
Nova Scotia	1 375	38 912	—
New Brunswick	194	62 730	438
Quebec	251	493 092	202 020
Ontario	20 065	467 298	425
Manitoba	2 271	153 191	220
Saskatchewan	5 942	87 521	11 432
Alberta	24 670	243 325	8 498
British Columbia	13 103	545 672	—
Yukon	—	109 521	100 787
North West Terr.	—	88 000	416 014

Figure 23-1.   The findings of the 1968 Canada Timberland Inventory.

23-2.   Use the data given in Figure 23-1 to construct equal area circles on a map of Canada representing the forested area in each province. Divide them[5] according to the headings given in the table. Could you suggest why so much of Quebec's forested area is not suitable for regular harvesting? A clue: look at the make-up of Quebec's forests on the natural vegetation map in your atlas, and look at the latitude of most of it. The farther north you go, the longer it takes trees to grow. It might take a pine in the latitude of James Bay 100 years to grow 8 metres.

Only 65 percent of Canada's forested land has been accurately inventoried. The land areas are so vast and the access to much of it so difficult and expensive that research is continually under way as to how the job might best be done by remote sensing. Air photography and satellite observations offer fruitful fields for developing new and more accurate techniques. Vegetation colour, shadows cast, and vegetation density can be read off photographs directly while infra-red photography will show how healthy the trees are. A rule-of-thumb that the tree surveyors, called "cruisers," use is that a tree is only worth cutting if its trunk diameter at breast height is 5 cm or more. In addition, an area should contain a certain density of such trees. One on its own is no good, at least in the coniferous forest. In the deciduous forest of south-west Ontario, single selected hardwood trees such as black walnut are worthwhile investments because they can be used in very thin layers called veneers. In 1972 such a tree on one farm near Toronto was valued at several thousand dollars. The bid was made by a firm specializing in supplying veneers to the furniture industry.

One of the most serious problems faced by the forestry industry is the loss of valuable timber because of fires. The old fire-watching towers are now obsolete and aircraft patrols replace them. Aircraft can even bomb fires with water and parachute teams of firefighters to douse a small fire before it gets out of control. While most forest fires are caused by people, the forest area lost to such fires each year is quite small. This is because people-caused fires are usually accessible. It is the fires due to natural agencies such as lightning which consume most timber because such fires, when started in remote areas, often have a chance to get a good hold before they are spotted. When they are, there is still the problem of rushing men and materials to the spot.

Yukon	3 683 sq. km
Norh West Terrltories	2 768 sq. km
British Columbia	1 646 sq. km
Other provinces	1 338 sq. km
Canada total	9 435 sq. km

Figure 23-2. Areas of timberland destroyed by forest fire (all causes) 1969.

The basic products of the forest industry are listed in Figure 23-3.

Product	quantlty ln billion cubic meters
Logs and bolts	105.0
Pulpwood	61.2
Fuelwood	6.1
Poles and pilings	0.4
Round mining timber	0.2
Charcoal wood	0.1
Fence posts	0.8
Fence rails	0.02
Miscellaneous timber	0.4

Figure 23-3. The basic products of the Canadian forestry industry, 1969.

23-3. Devise your own method of showing the information in Figure 23-3.

Most provinces of Canada have had increases in the amount of wood that has been cut for all purposes. The population of Canada continues to grow and the number of houses increases each year, the demand for paper of all types has been soaring, and foreign countries also have been adding their demands to those of Canadians for more and more timber and timber products.

Province	volume of wood cut 1966	1969
Newfoundland	98.8	83.2
Prince Edward I.	6.7	5.6
Nova Scotia	106.8	121.2
New Brunswick	195.3	236.4
Quebec	935.7	1 060.1
Ontario	567.1	621.6
Manitoba	42.5	52.9
Saskatchewan	45.4	82.1
Alberta	126.6	145.8
British Columbia	1 533.1	1 890.1
Yukon and N. W. T.	2.7	4.8
Canada total	3 660.7	4 303.8

Figure 23-4. The changes in the volume of wood cut in Canada by province over the four years 1966-1969 inclusive. Units are in millions of cubic feet.

23-4. Calculate the percentage change in the volume of wood cut between 1966 and 1969 inclusive for each province and for the Canada total. Express the results in the form of a bar graph[1] calculating how much more or how much less than the Canadian average (0 on the graph) each province's change has been. The figure each bar represents is therefore obtained by subtracting Canada's percentage from the percentage change of each of the provinces.

Compare eastern Canada with western Canada by shading eastern provinces red and the western provinces green (including the Yukon and the North West Territories with the western provinces.) What pattern do you see? Note: eastern Canada stops at Ontario's western boundary.

Obviously, some woods are much more valuable than others. After all, different woods are often used for different purposes. Some purposes may be much more in demand than others and so buyers will compete with each other and push up the price.

Tree species	value ($ million)	quantity (volume units)
Spruce	395.8	4 580 452
Douglas Fir	184.5	1 784 319
Hemlock	187.1	1 906 858
Cedar	104.3	857 712
White Pine	35.8	288 058
Lodgepole Pine	32.3	381 914
Jack Pine	29.0	355 434
Maple	27.9	209 771
Yellow Birch	19.5	140 413
Balsam Fir	12.6	146 620

Figure 23-5. The most significant lumber trees felled in Canada, 1969.

Figure 23-5 shows the most important trees cut in Canada as measured by their volume and value. Many hardwood trees (such as black walnut) are cut and worth considerably more than softwoods but they form only an insignificant part of the total, even though single trees may be worth thousands of dollars.

Province	Population (thousands)	lumber cut 1969 volume units	value ($ thousand)
Newfoundland	520	10 453	1 192
Prince Edward I.	110	3 780	87
Nova Scotia	785	206 834	16 654
New Brunswick	630	320 416	29 918
Quebec	6 000	1 705 523	143 370
Ontario	7 400	840 938	83 186
Manitoba	980	40 333	2 501
Saskatchewan	900	98 689	8 595
Alberta	1 620	429 133	33 980
British Columbia	2 100	7 438 515	737 968
Yukon and N.W.T.	50	5 743	616

Figure 23-6.   Lumber production and value by province, 1969.

The value of wood per unit volume of wood cut also varies provincially. This time it could be because of the fact that not every province has the same forest structure. The tree cover will vary as the soil and climatic conditions vary and these are very different from province to province.

Well, so far so good. We know something about the forest resources of Canada as a whole, as well as in the various provinces. We also know a little about some of the basic forest products and we also know which are the more valuable species of trees. Let us now take a cursory look at some other timber products besides sawn and shaped lumber.

Paper. Vast quantities of timber are made into paper. Of course, there are varying grades of paper, and the better grades are naturally worth more since they are made of better materials and cost more labour to produce. Generally, paper is made of a mat of wood fibres packed together while wet and then dried. To achieve a good writing surface, a clay is added. The clay is called kaolin and is white in colour besides being made of very fine particles. It glazes the surface of a sheet of paper so that it will take ink without splotching.

The raw material from which paper is made is called pulp. That is a good name for it. It is a mixture of wood fibres obtained by grinding wood and adding water, as well as a few chemicals to bleach it white. Pulp can be used to make a great variety of papers, from tissues to kraft paper and from fine writing paper to newsprint. The production of pulp in Canada in 1969 was as follows:

Quebec	6 547	tonnes
Ontario	3 961	tonnes
British Columbia	4 879	tonnes
Others	3 203	tonnes
Total	18 590	tonnes

Interestingly enough, Prince Edward Island produces no pulp at all. Why would that be? Figure 23-7 gives the breakdown of Canada's paper production for 1969.

Pulp production 1969

Quebec	6 547 000 tonnes
Ontario	3 961 000 tonnes
British Columbia	4 879 000 tonnes
Other provinces	3 203 000 tonnes
Canada total	18 590 000 tonnes

Paper production 1969

Newsprint	quantity	8 863 000 tonnes
	value	1 114 707 000 dollars
Book and writing paper	quantity	731 000 tonnes
	value	206 686 000 dollars
Total paper	quantity	12 093 000 tonnes
	value	1 733 151 000 dollars

Exports 1970

	U.K.		U.S.		All countries	
	tonnes	$ thousand	tonnes	$ thousand	tonnes	$ thousand
Pulp	377 385	49 540	3 315 519	485 453	5 581 325	785 229
Newsprint	411 665	59 596	6 212 134	872 544	8 090 007	1 110 393

Figure 23-7.   Selected data for the pulp and paper industry in Canada, 1969 and 1970.

23-7.   Which is worth more: newsprint or book and writing paper? Suggest why the cost per tonne of newsprint bought by the U.S. is less than that paid by the U.K. What percentage of Canada's paper production is newsprint? What percentage of Canada's pulp exports by weight is exported to the U.S.? Construct a divided bar graph[2] to show exports by destination of pulp and another divided bar to show the export by destination of newsprint. Use quantities, not values, for this.

And that's about it. Although forests are renewable resources, it is generally the policy of lumber and paper companies to grow trees so that they provide more and better timber more quickly than they do in the wild. This involves the careful planting of saplings which have been nursed from seed. The branches are cut off lower down the trunk as soon as practical. This means that knots are kept to a minimum and the timber is therefore stronger and easier to work with. Spraying trees to get rid of pests such as the spruce budworm is quite common. As a matter of fact, the federal government and the timber companies co-operate in the development of new and better ways to produce timber. Two research laboratories, one at Vancouver and the other at Ottawa, conduct research into soils, pests, surveying techniques, natural and artificial regeneration of cut-over lands, and the best ways to harvest timber from an area so that not all the trees are taken at any one time. This would mean that wildlife are not driven from an area and also it does not become an eyesore. Even better, soil erosion is kept to a minimum. It takes the best part of 1000 years to produce 2 cm of soil.

Somewhere else in this book it is said that Canada possesses some 22 percent of the world's softwood resources. Considering that Canada has less than 1 percent of the world's population, you have some idea of the great natural wealth that it represents. Yet this wealth is not infinite. It can easily be plundered — as it was in the past — and recovery is a long, slow process that takes several generations. For instance, a forest fire might last for a few hours. Yet the damage to the vegetation might take a century for nature to repair. Even with man's best intentions, trees grow at their own pace. Somehow, to achieve the highest sustainable yields from our forests, Canadians need more research facilities. After all, we really have only touched on one way in which Canada's trees can be used. There are many others even now. For example, they can be used as recreation areas, as hunting areas, and as wildlife conservation areas. Who knows what demands the future might make?

Appendices

Appendix 1. Bar graph. It may be vertical or horizontal. A **histogram** is vertical and the bars touch.

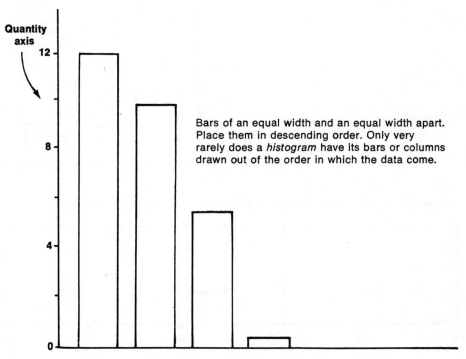

Bars of an equal width and an equal width apart. Place them in descending order. Only very rarely does a *histogram* have its bars or columns drawn out of the order in which the data come.

Identification of bars takes place along this axis.

Appendix 2. Compound or divided bar graph. Again, it may be vertical or horizontal. Each bar shows three variables in this example.

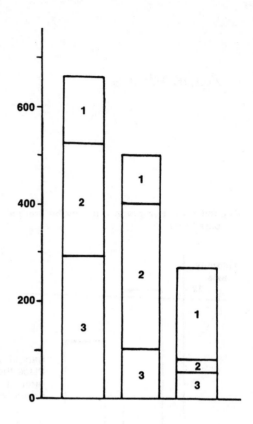

Appendix 3. A percentage bar graph. Data in percent must total 100 percent.

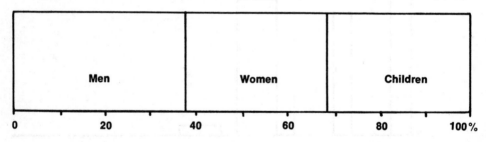

148

Appendix 4.   Proportional circles.

raw data	s.r. number (square root)		circle radius
100	10	make the circle	10 mm
400	20	radii proportional	20 mm
900	30	to the s.r. numbers	30 mm

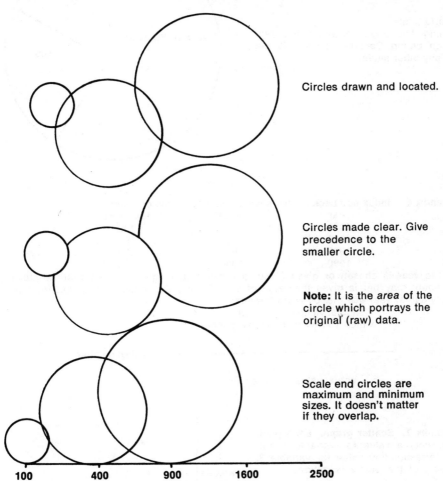

Circles drawn and located.

Circles made clear. Give precedence to the smaller circle.

Note: It is the *area* of the circle which portrays the original (raw) data.

Scale end circles are maximum and minimum sizes. It doesn't matter if they overlap.

100   400   900   1600   2500

149

Appendix 5. Divided circle. Each sector is in proportion to the whole circle.

$$\frac{\text{Canada total}}{\text{World total}} \times 360° \text{ is the formula for}$$

finding the angle between the radii which bound Canada's sector. Repeat for any other sector.

Appendix 6. Index numbers. They show percentage rates of change.

year	raw data	index number
1960	300	100
1970	580	193
1980	900	300
1990	1800	600

A base year is chosen or given (1960) and the actual figure for that year (whatever the figure may be) is given the value of 100. To find the index number for any later or any earlier year use the following formula:

$$\frac{\text{actual value for the year for which you want the index number}}{\text{actual value for base year}} \times 100 = \text{index number}$$

Appendix 7. Scatter graph. Each point represents a value for variable 1 and the corresponding value for variable 2. Naming of the points is optional.

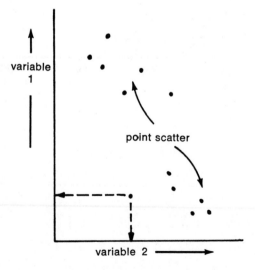

Appendix 8. Multiple-line, time-series graph. It is best to identify the lines by writing along them as shown.

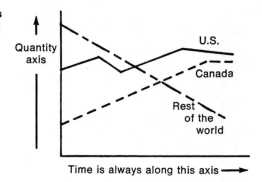

Time is always along this axis ⟶

Appendix 9. Compound line graph. Quantity intercepts on the vertical axis are cumulative. Therefore one reads the graph by examining the areas between the lines.

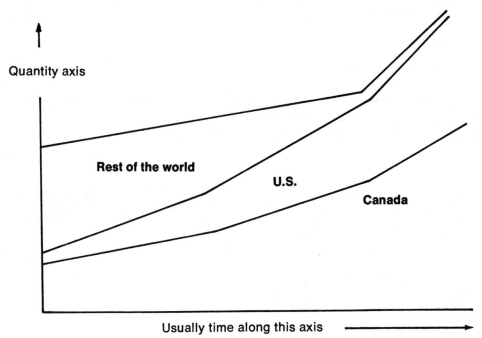

Usually time along this axis ⟶

151

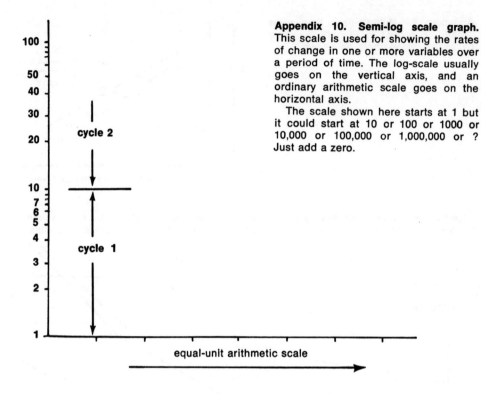

Appendix 10. Semi-log scale graph. This scale is used for showing the rates of change in one or more variables over a period of time. The log-scale usually goes on the vertical axis, and an ordinary arithmetic scale goes on the horizontal axis.

The scale shown here starts at 1 but it could start at 10 or 100 or 1000 or 10,000 or 100,000 or 1,000,000 or ? Just add a zero.

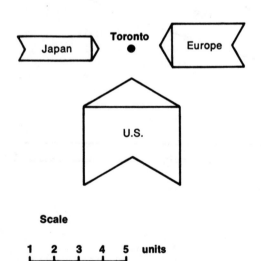

Appendix 11. Proportional-width arrows. Width is directly proportional to quantity. Arrows must be oriented correctly as far as is possible.

Appendix 12. Linear scale dispersion diagram. The scale is arithmetical and there is free choice over the scale values. They must span the full range of the data, however.

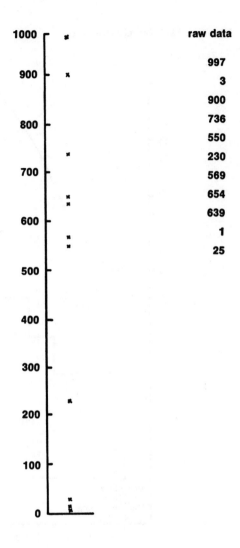

raw data

997
3
900
736
550
230
569
654
639
1
25

Appendix 13. The climate graph.

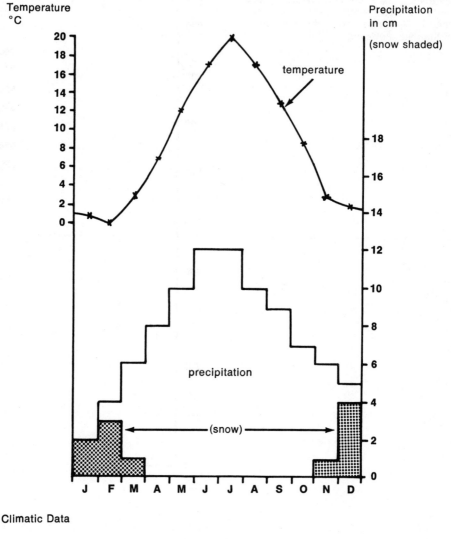

Climatic Data

	J	F	M	A	M	J	J	A	S	O	N	D
temperature °C	1	0	3	7	12	17	20	17	13	9	3	2
precipitation cm	2	4	6	8	10	12	12	10	9	7	6	5
(of which snow)	(2)	(3)	(1)	—	—	—	—	—	—	—	(1)	(4)

Note: precipitation bars are always drawn in the form of a histogram.[1]
It does not matter if the temperature line runs into the precipitation bars.

Appendix 14. Graded shading. In this example, 5 shades of one colour show 5 ranges of values. Try not to mix colours unless they flow into one another, e.g., yellows — oranges — reds blues — purples.

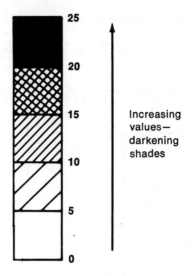

Increasing values— darkening shades

Area A has a value of 5
Area B has a value of 2

Appendix 15. Raised area maps.

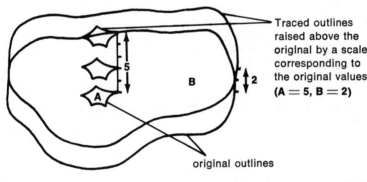

Traced outlines raised above the original by a scale corresponding to the original values
(A = 5, B = 2)

original outlines

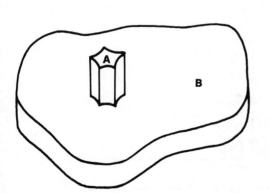

Construction lines removed. Note that A protrudes only 3 units above B now (A = 5, B = 2, A — B = 3)

155

Appendix 16.   Cumulative percentage curve.

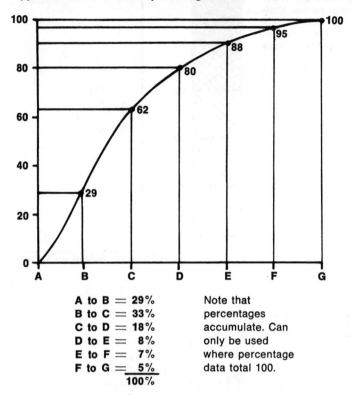

A to B = 29%	Note that
B to C = 33%	percentages
C to D = 18%	accumulate. Can
D to E = 8%	only be used
E to F = 7%	where percentage
F to G = 5%	data total 100.
100%	

Appendix 17.   Overlapping bars (bar groups).   For showing different quantities at a series of different times.

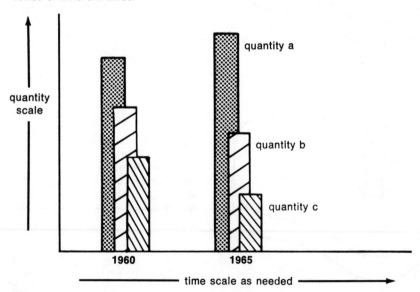

Appendix 18. Flow line diagram (flow bands). For showing the movements of various quantities in such a way that the width of the line (band) is proportional to the quantity being moved along that section.

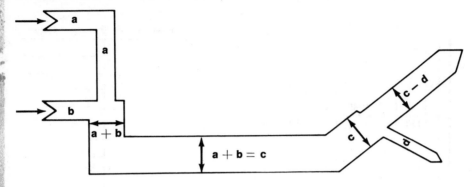

Appendix 19. Hythergraphs. For comparing the climates of two or more places on the same graph.

temperature °C

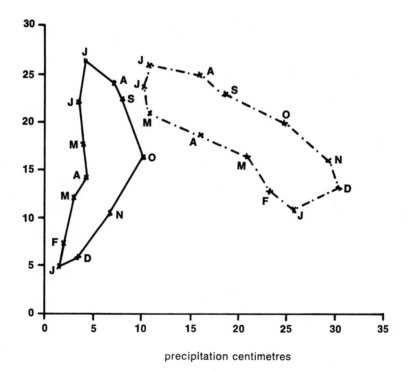

precipitation centimetres

Appendix 20. Positive-negative bar graphs. These are constructed vertically if plotting data in a time-series, but may be constructed horizontally if plotting data for a uniform time.

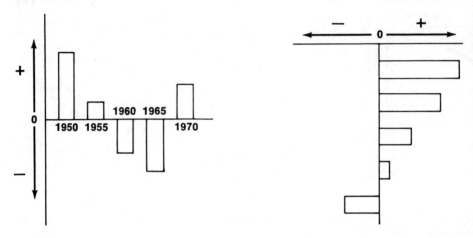